PAMELA HIRSCH

More Then Than Now

STONE TROUGH

BOOKS

REMEMBERING
PHIL AND OUR PARENTS

© Pamela Hirsch 2016
ISBN 978-0-9929497-4-7

Published by Stone Trough Books
The Old Rectory
Settrington
York YO17 8NP

Printed by CPI Antony Rowe Ltd, Chippenham, Wiltshire

Contents

Illustrations

A Childhood Time

TIME STOOD STILL in the Dales for some twenty years after the signing of the 1918 Armistice. In Europe, time rumbled forward, initiating unimagined horrors, but not much changed on the small stock farms tucked in under the Yorkshire Moors and adjacent to some water course. Apart from a shortage of men, everything went on as before.

The quiet in the Dales was immense in those days. It was the seasons that ordered our lives, rather than the clock. No tractors, all self-sufficiency achieved by horse, man and dog.

In memory, all winters were long and hard. Summers were alight with a sun that warmed the stone flags in our garden, too hot for bare feet and knees.

Februaries, still deep in snow, brought the harsh, dry call of a dog fox; in March, we watched, breathless, as hares boxed in the river fields. In April, there were new born lambs. In May the men had the laborious job of hoeing the roots, but for us children there were carpets of bluebells and anemones in the woods, followed by bird cherry and clusters of foxglove, like miniature cathedral spires, shadowed under the trees.

Meadowsweet, pink campion and hare bells, honeysuckle and vetches, sorrel, cow parsley and salad burnett burgeoned on the river bank, their scent like good wine. Bumblebees of every variety hummed and buzzed lazily, their over-filled pollen sacks weighing them down.

Mummy's little rose garden was edged with Mrs Sinkin's pinks. We could smell their distinctive scent while we lazed or had tea in the dappled shade under two old Keswick apple trees on the bottom lawn, and idly watched our elders playing tennis on the grass court above.

In late June or July came hay time, the meadows were striped in rows of mown grass, drying in the sun. When ready, it was made into pikes, each man using a long-handled fork with two curved tines; skilled work, whereby, if it rained, the water would roll off the top of the pike and run down the sides, not spoiling the dry hay within.

One year there was a whirlwind in the valley. Carefully built pikes were tossed into the sky, so thick in the air it became dark and threatening. The hay was thrown into the branches, and God knows where else, the entire crop lost. A freak storm that only happened once.

Carting the hay required wooden-wheeled, flat carts with sloping gates attached each end. One man would toss the hay from the pike on to the cart, while the other, standing on the cart, spread it evenly and kept it level. When it was some ten feet high, they roped the load securely. Another horse was needed to pull it back up to the farm, where it was forked again off the cart and into the lofts above the low mistals where the cattle were wintered.

My brother Phil and I would ride the second horses from stable to field. My short legs stretched horizontal across the broad, undulating back, I breathed in the delicious smell of sun-hot horse, felt his steady pace and his soft shiny coat against my skin. Phil knew how to release the animals from their stalls. It was he who helped me up, then climbed like a monkey on the other.

Arrived in the field, we slipped to the ground and one of the men would lift me up so I could catch hold of the ropes securing the hay, and scramble the rest, to ride up on top of it all the way home. Everything swayed and rocked through the steep gateways—it was like being out at sea on a rough day. We had to grab the ropes and hang on for dear life. In memory there was always sun beating down on our heads, and tiny specks of vibrating skylarks singing their hearts out, way above in the high bowl of blue sky, and it was glorious.

This was the time when the mown meadows re-grew grass, which was known as 'fog grass'. Miss Mudd, famous for winning prizes at every local show with butter sculptures, bought in milk from cows that had grazed on the fog because it was perfect for making her Blue Wensleydale cheese that must be eaten at Christmas.

In later years I lived near Miss Mudd and she kindly allowed me to watch the process. Her niece Frances told me that when she lived with her aunt, they would be sitting warm in the parlour some particularly cold evening, and Miss Mudd would spring up, "Oh my poor cheeses! Come along Frances, it is too cold for them in the cheese room!" and the two of them would lift each and every Blue Wensleydale into the parlour where there was still the glow of the dying fire, and then, next day, return them to the cheese room.

I will never forget the creamy and delicious flavour of Miss Mudd's Blue Wensleydale cheese. We always had one for Christmas, and today's version is not a patch on the original.

August or early September was harvest time. A horse pulled the mower that cut the crop, starting at the outside of the field and working inwards until there was just a small island of standing corn left in the middle. Then everyone would go down armed with sticks and clubs to circle round it.

When the mower started again, hundreds of fat rabbits bolted out across the field and the men despatched as many as they could. When he was old enough to have a gun, Phil shot them. We felt safe with Phil but I saw Dad's face tighten with apprehension when old Mr Abbott appeared, bent double with arthritis, horizontal from the hips, manoeuvring himself into the circle. He came from nowhere, always just in time, and always got a rabbit to take home for his dinner. Old Mr Abbott, a great church-goer, was stone deaf and sat in front. When the parson chose to skip a few verses in very long hymns, Mr Abbott's sonorous voice continued to soar through every verse, and we all had to wait for him to finish. On one occasion he read the lesson as follows:

"hand 'e 'ung by the 'airs hov 'is 'ead hon the booze hof han hoak!" Absalom? I can't remember, but we were all reduced to helpless laughter.

I joined in the circle surrounding those poor bolting rabbits, I didn't mind this sudden slaughter as I was old enough to understand the damage rabbits caused the farm, and their death was instantaneous and provided good meat for the men; it was the snares that haunted me.

In those days most hill farmers set snares, or had some man to do it for them. The snares were a loop of copper wire attached to a peg. Rabbits were so numerous that it was quite easy to find their 'runs'. If you have ever heard a rabbit scream, it is something you never forget. The wire of those snares drew tighter and tighter round the neck of the rabbit and its death was long and painful.

Dad employed a man to snare the farm, and I followed him. Every evening I pulled the noose tight and wrapped it round its peg, making each trap harmless.

If the man told Dad what I was up to, Dad never said anything to me, but it was hard on the man, his only payment being what he caught.

To continue with the harvesting, the cut corn was left in the field for a few days to dry, then the horse-driven binder picked it up and tied it into sheaves. The men lifted the sheaves two at a time and to build them into stooks, each sheaf standing and leaning against another and eight to the stook.

Phil and I learned how to build stooks and were thrilled to think we were helping the men, but oh how scratchy the straw on our bare arms!

Our fear was that if we didn't get the balance right and our stook collapsed, the tired men would send us home saying they hadn't time to do things twice.

One year, it rained throughout the whole of August. Wet grain blackened in the stooks and sprouted. The whole crop was destroyed and useless, but normally, when sufficiently dry, it was carted to the lofts in the new barn that Grandpa's joiner, Sam Ingham, had designed and built to last for ever. Its lofts were divided by a gap and some weeks later the threshing machine rolled up and parked in the gap.

Threshing day was a great occasion. Don, the farm manager, stood on top of the thresher to receive the sheaves, and cut the string before feeding them into the machine. Len and Charlie forked the sheaves down from the high lofts each side. Jack was in charge of changing the sacks that filled so rapidly with the grain. The beating noise of the thresher was deafening, the dust and straw everywhere, you couldn't hear yourself speak.

At the end of the day, the loose straw had to be forked back and up into the lofts for winter bedding, the heavy sacks of grain carried, across the shoulders, up stone steps to another loft for storage.

By this time the hay fields had re-grown masses of grass. If there were not enough mouths to eat it, Dad would take Don and Jack in the car to Otley Market and purchase a few cross-bred steers. He then went to the mill in Bradford leaving the men to drive his purchases the ten mile journey home.

Sometimes they didn't turn up till next day. They explained the beasts were difficult to drive, or that there was fog on the moor, and Dad always accepted the story, but with a smile. He well knew of the pub en route, and in those days pubs always had a barn or a yard to rest drovers' cattle, and the drovers themselves slept in the bar.

This was my childhood time, and I thought my life would always be thus, just the same, for ever.

Family Background

On father's side of the family we were nineteenth-century émigrés from Germany, but this was not discussed with us children. We knew our surname was German and that Uncle Phil, Dad's elder brother, was a hero who won a Victoria Cross in the First World War, but I don't remember any of us asking to be told about the war and Dad never mentioned it.

In spite of his built-up shoe, we knew Dad as a vigorous and cheerful individual who could do absolutely everything; he played a fierce game of tennis, albeit in his own inimitable style, and I believe was a very good golfer.

It was some fifty years later that I learned Great Grandfather had come from Germany and settled in Aberdeen to trade fine woollen cloths between the two countries. The business had thrived and expanded until his accountant, whom he had befriended and trusted, ran off with all the money. He never employed anyone again, but continued what business he could manage as a sole trader.

When Great Grandfather died, his widow and sons moved south to Leeds and Harry, the elder, who became our grandfather, started a woollen business, with partners in Bradford.

The younger brother, our great uncle Dave, married Evelyn, whom we all thought extremely elegant but rather distant and not often seen. They found the abuse caused by their German name at the time of the War too much to bear and became Mr and Mrs High, which we knew Grandpa didn't like.

Grandpa Harry married Edith Brindley in the 1890s. She was one of a large Leeds family manufacturing glassware, with close connections to the Boyles and Richardsons, and they had three children. Phil, the eldest, was born in 1896 followed by Dad (Frank) in 1898 and Marjorie a year or two later.

It was only in his very old age that Dad told me a little of their childhood adventures. We drove into Leeds some years ago and found the house where they had lived in Park Square, and later another house a little further from the town centre.

Dad described how when very small he and Phil shared a room. They would wake early and try to slip from the house, but never managed it. Their grandmother slept in the next room and never failed to spring up and bar their escape. He didn't like his grandmother, but her portrait that used to hang by the turn of the stairs here, revealed a charming woman with a smile, and soft curls peeping from under some frilly headdress. But now I will never know why Dad didn't care for her.

When in their teens, Grandpa gave Phil and Frank an old Renault sports car they called 'The Streak,' and on one memorable occasion its brakes failed going down Scott Hill Road in Leeds, at the bottom of which trams were crossing to and fro. The car gathered speed and shot in between them, then somehow got into the tram lanes and they couldn't get out of them. Tears of laughter ran down Dad's old face as he told me the story.

On another occasion the boys were sent to collect the 'Lanchester' from its factory where it had been returned due to the pneumatic tyres puncturing every few miles. The designer decided the car's tyres should be protected with canvas covers, but in the event the canvas rubbed even worse than the road surface, and before the boys arrived home, every tyre was flat. I believe the Lanchester was brought out at much the same time as Rolls Royce. Grandpa had considered them both and sadly made the mistake of choosing the Lanchester above the Rolls.

Frank worshipped Phil and never deemed himself as gifted, but both boys were intelligent. When the time came, Phil won an Exhibition to both Oxford and Cambridge, and a year or so later Frank followed with his Exhibition to Cambridge.

World War One intervened in all their plans. Instead of going to university, Uncle Phil joined up and was immediately sent to an OTC (Officers Training Camp), and Dad could hardly wait to follow.

Phil was aware of this and in his letters home both to his parents and to Frank himself he stressed that Frank must wait for his eighteenth birthday before joining up, and on no account volunteer as a 'Tommy'—but to no avail.

As soon as he finished school, he and his favourite cousin, Basil Richardson, fudged their ages and volunteered. They were just seventeen at the time, but no one checked up on their ages. The country was desperately short of men, and the two boys thought the war a marvellous adventure.

They had been at boarding school and were used to being away from home. Also, they were together and relied on each other, which was a big advantage over the lads who had never left home nor been far from where they were brought up.

Their short training continued in France and Dad described how he and Basil ventured into a French café and bought a bottle of cheap white wine. It was their first taste of alcohol and they thought it tasted foul, but downed the bottle in no time and thought life hilarious. "French piss!" said one and both found the remark witty, adult and marvellously funny. It still made Dad laugh when he told me the story in his late nineties, but tears were not far away.

15

Shortly after this Basil was sent to another company and it was only now, when they were separated, that the boys discovered they had almost nothing in common with the men around them. They experienced the horrors of trench warfare outside the bond of friendship and understanding that united the less privileged lads and was so vital for survival.

Phil wrote letter after letter to the authorities, desperately trying to get permission for Frank to join his company but in spite of pulling many strings the plan failed.

Almost immediately, Dad was appallingly wounded, half a knee shot away—and he lay in the wet mud of a ditch under the remains of a little copse, the battle continuing all round him, and was shot again in the shoulder.

No one noticed he was missing. He lay in the mud and mayhem for four days. He told me later that he remembered being able to reach a few leaves which he sucked, trying to quench his thirst.

His company was sent down the line to rest, and an officer leading its replacement went forward, searching for the placements of the enemy, especially their snipers. He found Dad by chance, still hanging on to life by a thread.

Dad was carried to a Field Station and its surgeon knew he should amputate the leg above the knee, but could not bring himself to do it. He spent the whole night trying to patch up what was left of the knee, and I wish that someone in our family could have traced who he was and thanked him.

Dad spent months in a French hospital, too ill to be moved back to England, and Uncle Phil managed to visit him briefly, and told him how lucky he was to be out of the war, as he then believed! When eventually Dad was strong enough to be moved to England he landed up in the Fishmonger's

Guild Hall in London, which was being used as a hospital.

The remarkable head matron expected all her patients to stand to attention by their beds when she entered a ward, and of course Dad couldn't even get out of bed. She harangued him loudly for this 'lack of respect,' and old Dad laughed again, remembering her indignation.

Basil visited Dad, on leave from France, before catching a train north, his last leave, a painful memory. Dad was appalled to see his kilt was covered in dried mud and half of it shot away. Shortly afterwards he learned that Basil had been killed.

When well enough to be sent home to convalesce, Dad was told he would never walk again, and I asked him how he had set about disproving the verdict.

"Oh," he said, "I just got out of bed every day and tried to take a step or two, and the leg swelled up, but I kept at it, and in the end I found I could walk, anyway with a stick." There was no mention of pain, never in all the years I knew him.

He went to Cambridge University as soon as he could and decided to study medicine. He thought it the best career for someone so handicapped. Every day the newspapers listed the names of men killed, wounded or missing. Cambridge was practically empty. Phil, his beloved brother, was named among the dead and awarded a posthumous V.C.

Dad could not bear to continue alone in Cambridge. He got on a train and went to the depot of the Green Howards, his brother's regiment, and asked if they could find him a job. On learning that he was Uncle Phil's brother, they received him warmly and sent him to an OTC Camp for a month. He was then posted back France, on 'light duties', i.e. not in the fighting line, and to the Durham Light Infantry rather than the Green Howards.

He couldn't walk without a stick but, arriving at their depot, he found several officers grouped round a table, too exhausted to be even aware of his presence. He asked what he could do to help and, without taking in his condition, one of them said he had better go up the line, and see what he could do to help. They had lost nine officers in the line the night before.

Dad must have ridden up to the front line, carrying his rifle and his stick, and it was madness. He got himself into a trench with the greatest difficulty and realised he could never get out of it, neither move forward nor back. He could do nothing to help the tired men preparing for yet another onslaught from the enemy.

There was a terrible battle that night, which I believe was actually the last of the war, and through the slow, unending hours, Dad waited and watched, terrified and helpless. He heard the cries of the wounded in no man's land, saw in the flares of light Roman Catholic priests tending the dying. He heard the murmured prayers when there was a lull in the fighting. Expecting his own death at any moment, he wished that he too had been born a Catholic. And yet, as a boy, he had been brought up to cross the road rather than acknowledge the presence of someone known to be Roman Catholic!

My eldest sister Dee, now in her nineties, tells me that Dad avenged his brother's death that night, but Dad never said anything about that to me. Sadly this part of his Army service remains unrecorded in official reports. Neither the Green Howards nor Durham Light Infantry offices have been able to trace any record of what happened when he returned to France. Nonetheless when my nephew Jarvis and I went to Arras to trace the last days of Uncle Phil's life, our excellent guide, Jonathan Nicholls, a published authority on all battles in the region of Arras in both World Wars, undertook more research for Dad, and found enough evidence to vouch that what Dad told me is true.

Mother came from a musical family, and was the youngest and much loved child with three elder brothers. When the second eldest boy joined up, their mother moved the family to wherever he was posted like 'camp followers,' and they finished up in a flat in Cambridge.

They were impoverished gentry. Grandpapa was a musician, a modest composer and player of the organ. He had been left a legacy large enough for himself, but it was very stretched for a family of six! Mother often spoke of the flat, which over-looked King's College, and also of her beloved father's "unworldliness."

On one occasion he met a family friend in the street who unburdened herself, naming endless aches and pains, and Grandpapa waited patiently till the end, when he touched his hat and said how glad he was that she was well. His mind, had been miles away, he hadn't heard a word!

In spite of straitened circumstances it was a happy family, and the children attended a little old Dame school nearby. They survived the First World War almost unscathed. Mother was eighteen when it ended.

The eldest brother, Uncle Arthur, wounded the day before the Germans used mustard gas for the first time and therefore fortunate to have survived at all, worked in London and in later years was in charge of King's Cross Station. He met my elder sisters en route to their boarding school near Reading, wearing a top hat, dress coat and smart black walking stick, and they felt very important to be thus escorted to the correct platform.

It was in Cambridge that father and mother met, and I wonder now whether he had returned to Cambridge with the idea of continuing his course at the university, but mother and he fell in love and married, in Cambridge, a year or so later.

Mummy's other two brothers returned from France and like many others could find no work now the war was over, so they joined a Government-sponsored scheme to help to develop Kenya, and went out there to farm coffee.

Mother was particularly close to the elder brother, Forest, and missed him dreadfully. Everyone loved him and, had he been able to stay in England, he would have been her 'rock' to lean on in the very different circumstances her marriage brought. He told us that the Africans who worked for him gave him the nickname of "Peppery" but in reality he was the kindest of men, highly respected by all who knew him. His workers were fond of him and very loyal.

Although Dad's family home was in Leeds and the wool firm in Bradford, our parents chose to live in the country, and in 1921 our Yorkshire grandfather gave them Low Hall as a wedding present.

Finding Low Hall was a piece of luck. They had seen an advertisement for a property called Carr Lodge but could not find it, and they stopped to ask directions from an old man leading his equally aged white horse up Thornthwaite Bank.

"Ye'ere only a few 'undred yards from Carr Lodge," he said, "boot I've 'eard 'ow Low 'all ist ont' market too, an' I reckon ye'll like it better. Lo'all's a grand place, ye should go and see it fust before ye look at Carr Lodge."

They were so confident in the old man's opinion, they did as he directed, and fell so completely for Low Hall and its little farm that they never thought of checking out Carr Lodge.

Perhaps for Dad living in the Dales was the panacea he needed after his horrific war experience, and our mother's delight in Low Hall must, I believe, have boosted her courage, in surroundings and people so far removed from the genteel life she knew in Cambridge, its beautiful architecture, and the music that meant so much to her.

The farm was, and is, a typical Dales farm of one hundred and fifty acres. The house lies in the bottom of the valley, just above the river, where there are some thirty acres of good land, stretching south. The rest is made up of steep, small fields, bounded by dry stone walls. Streams and springs are everywhere.

Forty acres of mature woodland is carpeted with bluebells every Spring. A further few acres of rocks, reeds and bog transforms itself in May when old, silver-barked, craggy hawthorns crown their every branch with exquisite white blossom and its all pervading scent. It becomes a veritable fairy land for one short month, and as lovely again under heavy snow.

Our family differed from our neighbours, in that we were neither estate owners, nor tenants, nor of the local farming community. We were 'incomers, neither fish nor fowl,' and our having a German-Jewish surname was seriously prejudicial for our parents so soon after the First World War.

Apart from one or two exceptions, we children had few close friends but we weren't aware of loneliness. Our lives centred round family and the farm. We didn't attend the village school; when the time came we went to Harrogate schools.

Dad had masses of business friends in Bradford but our mother hardly knew them. The wool trade had flourished in the war, and the wives of the young mill owners were rich,

21

fashionably dressed, tough, sharp and gregarious. Among them mother was an outsider, her background in Cambridge had been one of genteel poverty, high Anglican Church and its music.

Unfortunately Dad had not a note of music in him, so mother was unaware of the very live music 'circles' in and around Leeds, where she might have found more compatible friends.

Her rejection of Bradford society must have curtailed Dad's social life, but he accepted the 'divide' and made the most of lunching at the Union Club. Nearly all the mill owners lunched there and played snooker before returning to their desks. Enormous business deals were agreed at the snooker tables. Thousands and thousands of pounds were bought and sold on a handshake, the wool bought would be delivered next morning and a signed cheque returned with the lorry.

Dad described this to me years later and smiled, savouring the memory of friendship and trust it had brought into his life; the unspoken and unbroken integrity. I remember asking if the members clubbed together to help in the event of a business 'going down,' and his response: "Yes," he said, "always if we could."

I believe mother was lonely at first. Her in-laws loved her dearly, but in those days sixteen to twenty miles was enough to keep people apart. There is a family record that she spread her first baby's nappies over lavender bushes to dry in the sunshine, which somehow conjures a picture of her spending long days on her own.

She was light-hearted, innately innocent and brave. Her constant desire to help others eventually created a small group of devoted friends and she later earned further local respect for being the first woman seen to drive her car through Dacre.

It was many years later, coming out of Darley church, that a very old woman said she had helped Mummy in the house for a period of some years. She told me that when her husband became seriously ill, Mum learned that the family could not go for their summer holiday because he could no longer drive the car.

"Don't cancel your booking," Mother said, "I'm sure there's a way round this."

On the day of departure the family waited to see who could come, and when Mummy rolled up driving the farm Land Rover, the invalid husband almost refused to get in. He couldn't believe a woman was capable of driving a Land Rover, little knowing that Mum had had to teach herself to drive both it and its trailer to take animals to market during the war when Dad had volunteered again and was in Italy.

It took over two hours to drive to Filey, but half way there they found a good picnic spot in a field and helped Mummy to unload the surprise picnic she had brought.

As the teller of this story continued, she would never forget the beautiful table-cloth Mummy spread out on the field, the napkins that followed, and how they, with the fine-cut delicious sandwiches, sausage rolls, the home-made sponge with lemon icing, the children's lemonade and huge thermos of tea, turned the day into an unforgettable occasion.

Mummy was no longer young at the time but she went to collect the family at the end of their week and continued to drive them both ways for the many years that followed.

Dad started the British Legion in our valley in 1924, and remained its president for over seventy years, and eventually served on almost every committee in the valley.

When he resigned from Gouthwaite Reservoir in the

Eighties, Pateley Bridge flooded for the first time in history, an unlikely coincidence that made us laugh.

He was an excellent judge of cattle but never a 'hands on' farmer. He employed five men to run the farm, and for us children these men were our friends and allies.

Don, a Highlander, was head stockman. A good-looking man with honest eyes and wonderful smile, he had had a splendid Scottish education and in later years when he and I worked together, he quoted Robbie Burns at me for hours on end! He was an excellent stockman and loved all young things whether animals or children, but he was superstitious and firmly believed that Low Hall was haunted.

He and Mrs Don lived in the new cottage that Grandpa and Dad built above—and far too close to—the Hall. A plain building but equipped with bath and indoor WC, with three bedrooms, it was of a much better standard than most, for those days. They had five children, all of whom were our friends, without ever entering each other's houses.

When Phil and I passed the cottage around noon we were almost blown away by the scent of frying onions emanating through the open door. Dad didn't like onions, so we rarely tasted them at home, and we felt it to be a serious loss.

Jack was Don's right-hand man and in charge of the farm when Don was absent at sales. Jack walked to work along the railway that ran through the farm. He was a bachelor for years, but in mid-life married a retired schoolmistress. Mrs Garbett was beautiful, a real gentlewoman, her manner quiet but firm. We all loved her and we loved Jack too. He was thin and angular, not a pick of fat on him, had been gassed in the war and had a slight stutter. In the early years, I firmly believed he couldn't get through a day's work without my assistance.

The pedigree bulls had a box each with solid black wooden doors. Don and Jack mucked them out every day and slung what water was left in the buckets through the doors and into the yard. I was about three when I met the full force of a gallon of cold water that nearly drowned me. My indignation was ridiculous. I reported the offence to Don as I walked back home, dripping wet and deeply offended. I refused Jack's apologies and it was Don who had the job of restoring an eventual peace and amity between us!

Dad started a herd of Beef Shorthorns, most of which he sourced from Scotland, and it wasn't long before he was taking on the Scots, sending promising young animals to be shown and sold in Perth and then exported to the Argentine.

My earliest memories are of seeing large iron buckets filled with cold water, commercial soap and scrubbing brushes which were all Don and Jack had to wash and groom the cattle ready for sale. It was all done by hand and took hours, but when at last they had curry-combed their thighs with backward strokes to create a wave, brushed out the tails and oiled the horns, the bulls looked wonderful. They were halter-led; no one dreamed of using nose-clips in those far off days.

The late summer grass soaked my bare legs and sandals as I followed the cavalcade being led across our fields to the village station, and watched the bulls stepping sedately into waiting trucks, knee deep in straw, and wishing fervently that I might go too. Don travelled with them and within a few hours they were comfortably installed in Perth Market.

Remembering it now brings home how much simpler, kinder and easier the system was not only for the cattle, but also the farmer, compared with the long, endless, cattle truck journeys on today's busy roads.

Len and Charlie helped with the stock, particularly the four carthorses, but were mainly engaged with the arable. The farm was nearly self supporting so far as feed was concerned.

Len walked from the other side of the river every morning, and has become an ambiguous figure, through time. He was a terrible grumbler, and I don't remember a family. Perhaps he was single, certainly he wasn't fond of children. Whenever Phil and I asked to be lifted on to a horse or into a cart he would say, "an' 'ool tek the blame if yer fall off?" He was courteous and a great worker, but we never got further than that; we had to ask Don and Jack for such treats.

"Charlie," Dad said, was "sixpence short of a shilling." One day riding home from school in Mum's car, we followed Charlie down the farm lane. The car had squeaky brakes, but Charlie, sitting in the old cart with its metal-bound, wooden wheels crunching on unmade road, had no idea we were behind him. He thought the squeaks a skylark, and gazed and gazed up into the sky to spot it, and I remember the boys and I nearly falling out of the car with laughter.

Charlie's wife, Mrs Upton, had a difficult time of it with both Charlie and their two small sons. She told Mother she had to lock up the baking in her wardrobe before coming out, as Charlie and the boys thought nothing of eating a week's supply in one go, and with wages at nineteen shillings a week, there was no chance of making more.

In school holidays, the boys came with their mother on Mondays, when Mrs Upton helped with laundry. They always arrived in a hurry and rather late, because, as she said, she had to "muck out the 'Royal Bath' first."

Mummy always laughed at this description of the local pub's facilities. In those days the Royal Oak possessed the only bath in the village, so, in a way, it was pretty grand.

One Monday the little boys were playing in the yard with an old piece of rope, and Mum asked if they were pretending to be horses

"Stallions!!" they retorted with scorn.

Not long ago, I was talking to an elderly stockman at the Great Yorkshire Show, and he revealed he was the elder of the two boys. He was head shepherd of a first-rate, well renowned flock in the Wolds, and I thought how proud dear Mrs Upton must be. I was particularly sad to hear she had died a month or two before, so I had only just missed the opportunity of seeing her again.

Our laundry was a new, one-storey building which replaced a beautiful barn, as old as the house, that was pulled down. It must, I think, have cast a deep cold shadow on the north side of the house, but the thought of it being demolished saddens me, as does the destruction of a little winding stone staircase, also taken out when Mr Wilson made his plans in 1921. The laundry was practical but a very plain building with incubator and coal shed on one side. There was a copper heater with a fire set under it for boiling the linen and similarly another fire underneath the iron heater, which was an iron box, with ridged sloping sides to keep the irons in place. Inevitably there was a mangle with wooden rollers and a large deal table padded with thick cotton cloth on which to use the irons. Whoever did the ironing stood on duck boards, and there was constant traffic between the table and the iron heater. I am amazed now that such perfect results were achieved by this archaic system!

Beyond the west end of the house near the laundry was the "drying green" where all the house linen was hung out to dry, and is now a rose garden, and beyond it was the vegetable garden which is much the same today as it was then. I can see Corrie, our cairn terrier, laying himself out out on the drying green under bright early sinshine, with an expectant look on his face. He knows our house cat is hunting down by the river. Soon she appears with a young rabbit almost as big as herself. It is a long steep haul for her to drag such a load back to the house, so she scrambles on the top of the dry stone wall and walks slowly but steadily on top of it, the body of the rabbit bumping along, dragging between her legs. At last she arrives and jumps nimbly on to the green dropping her trophy immediately in front of Corrie's nose. He pretends to ignore her presence, his eyes fixed on the rabbit. He has no intention of saying thank you. The cat doesn't deign to look at him, such a fat, lazy fellow that he is. He might as well have the rabbit, she doesn't want it. She departs, tail up, proud of herself, a superior being.

It was Bert who laid and lit the fires in the laundry on early Monday mornings. He also worked in the garden, fed the hens and chopped wood and brought in the coal. He was a very small, dear man, who lived in the old village above the farm.

He and his wife, Mrs Nelson, had two girls, Doris and Olga, who had been working in Darley laundry for some years before David was born. The poor girls had round, pale, faces from standing hour upon hour in all that hot steam, but David was the prettiest, pinkest, smiliest baby ever.

When Mrs Nelson came down to the Hall to help Mother with her annual jumble sale for Dr Barnardos, there was a problem of where to put young David.

"I haven't waited for him for all these years," she said, "to put him behind no doors."

Heaven knows where an appropriate place was found for

the pram. Our dining-room was already crowded out with jumble and buyers. It was wartime (World War II) and there was clothes rationing, so jumble sales were important, well attended events.

Mother allowed all her helpers to purchase one garment for themselves before the sale opened and told us laughingly that a terrible argument had arisen between two members both wanting to buy the same garment. To her embarrassment, and in the middle of the sale, the door opened, and Phil, aged about five, piped up, "Are Mrs B. and Mrs H. still 'squaddling' Mummy?"

Perhaps that was the day that Mrs Don spent sixpence on buying a tailcoat for Tommy. The coat, black and made of the finest wool cloth, would be something warm for him to wear. Tommy was an Irish casual labourer, helping on the farm, and temporarily housed in Don's cottage. He was so delighted with the gift, he put it on immediately and raced off to the Royal Oak to celebrate. The inn-keeper was up a ladder, cleaning the staircase window and saw his approach, black coat tails flying, He laughed so much, he fell off the ladder and broke his leg.

I see that staircase window when I walk down to the village today and the memory always makes me smile.

Some years after David's arrival Mrs Nelson produced another baby, and one sensed he was a somewhat unwanted addition to the family. He was a very plain little boy, but full of character, and at a young age he kept racing-pigeons.

Dad unwittingly shot his favourite pigeon and much to Bert's embarrassment Albert arrived at the back door with his father, demanding compensation, the poor dead dove in his hands. I think Dad was a bit embarrassed too, but ten shillings appeared to sort the matter out. However I will always remember the way Bert cuffed Albert on the head with his cap, saying, "Enoof o' that!!" knowing only too well that the little boy might take a chance of further bargaining.

Albert grew up into a grand sort of young man, he and one of the sisters came back to see me a few years ago, the sister also good-looking these days, but told me, sadly, that David had died.

Five Fledglings

SECURE AND WARM in my cot I sleep, and dreaming hear the murmur of a distant train. Now, its acceleration up the incline to woodlands. Nearer, nearer, bustling through trees. Nearer, louder! And the great, black, sweating engine hurtles towards me. Barred, trapped, I scream! And screaming...wake.

The above nightmare and two other equally terrifying dreams are my first memories and occurred before I could talk, so none of my family knew what it was that distressed me. Mystified, someone would hold me gently until I relaxed and slept once more.

I was born in 1929, ten years after the end of World War One and ten years before the start of World War Two, and I was the youngest of four children. Our family lived on a Dale's farm in North Yorkshire and a railway ran through the middle of its lands and far too close to the farmhouse and buildings. Wooden gates each side of the line were kept closed as much as possible, but this was difficult with the constant movement of men and animals to and from fields and buildings above and below.

Mrs Don, the farm manager's wife, kept an eagle eye on all us children, as well as her own five, and when I was about three she saw my two elder sisters and brother helping me to climb the ladder of the signal-box opposite her cottage. At the top they unfurled an umbrella with strings attached, and it dawned on her that they intended to use it as a parachute. The baby! she thought. Oh no! She was half way up the ladder herself before she saw the teddy-bear primed for the experiment.

I came back to live in Low Hall again in the late 1980s and have farmed here ever since. On my return I was to discover that the old house was in a state of serious disrepair, and unexpected visitors kept popping in to bring me unwished-for information.

First came the insurers . . . was I aware that the house and farm buildings were hopelessly under-insured?

Then the local builder . . . did I know that one of the three gable roofs was leaking?

The electrician called . . . he hoped that I realised the whole house needed rewiring. For years he had feared the place would burn down.

When the plumber came, he explained that all our water requirements ran through ancient lead piping sourced from a very unreliable spring in one of the top fields.

It wasn't all bad news because what transpired was a once-in-a-lifetime opportunity to take the interior of the house back to its sixteenth/seventeenth-century plan, and I had the luck to be in a position to do it.

Even more fortunate was the fact that when Grandpa engaged the Leeds architects William Hill & Son to modernise the interior in 1921, Mr Hill made and kept an exact plan of how he had found it. Had he not done so, I would have had no positive knowledge of its layout in the seventeenth century, stretching back perhaps as far as the fifteenth century.

Both the house and farm were Grandpa's wedding present to our parents, and we children grew up living in Mr Wilson's 1920's reinvention of the house, and we loved the place, every square inch of it.

We were born to its chill rooms and never thought twice about how dark they were. We looked through the high-set mullion windows and saw the beautiful Dale all round us, waiting for our explorations.

In summer time we swam in the Nidd and I don't remember feeling cold, but clearly recall my brother Phil being given a wonderful rubber ring in the form of a duck, and I was green with envy, dying to have a go myself. It was even more exciting to see both Phil and it turn turtle as they gathered speed in the current, Phil's legs waving in the air. In a flash Mother was waist deep in the river and had Phil in her arms but to my great disappointment the lovely duck sailed on. We children were unaware of any prejudice, but we had few friends in those early years. Our focus was our family and the five men who worked the farm. Perhaps Buffin, my perspicacious second sister, had a feeling we were different in some way. She was a small person with ginger curls and a pink-and-white complexion. We, her three siblings, were skinny and had dark hair...mine completely straight.

Buffin didn't take things for granted, she was very perceptive from an early age and didn't think life at Low Hall as perfect as we did. After a rather smart party that Dee and she had attended, she was heard to say,

"Well yes, they invited us, even though we are home-made girls."

None the less I don't think even Buffin appreciated the family's precarious finances in that time. It was years later, when we laughed at being told that local people used to say, "We can't make head nor tale of the Hirschs. One minute they are buying the most expensive perambulator and the next, cancelling the Radio Times!"

Wool like almost every other trade was hit by the great recession of the 1920's, but Dad, with his partner Johnnie

Rhodes, made a good team. They engaged 'sorters' to prepare the washed wool into attractive 'tops' for the spinners to buy.

Making 'tops' involves sorting the newly washed fleece into its several qualities or grades, the longest 'threads' being the most valuable. Dad's many 'sorters' worked on all four floors, throwing the separated wools down the appropriate holes from top to bottom of the building.

On one famous occasion a spinner arrived on the mill's fourth floor looking for Dad and, stepping back, vanished through a hole in the floor and shot through three more levels before landing on a huge pile of wool in the basement . . . unhurt! How lucky that the wool had not already been shipped away somewhere!

Hirsch & Son became Hirsch Son & Rhodes and the partnership thrived. Dad had offices in Toronto, Boston and Sidney as well as in London until he 'floated' the business in the 1950's.

*   *   *

When I came back in the late 1980s, my friend and well-known York architect, Alistair Haldane, came to look at the interior of the house, and we both fell in love with the original seventeenth-century century plan left by Mr Wilson. We spent a full six months swopping notes and drawings, working out how near we could come to re-instating it, long before the builders were even thought of.

The work took two years and through his gifts of patience and courtesy Mr Haldane managed to persuade the planners to agree to every insertion of new mullion and return of wall back to historic positions on the ground floor.

When the last lick of paint had dried, we had a party for the trades people and their wives, and it was wonderful. We were all on a high, the place looked marvellous and reflected the high standard of good workmanship, and the party was my way of thanking them.

For me there was an added joy. I sensed with utmost certainty that the spirit of the house itself rejoiced with us, that it was glad to find itself back in the old, familiar pattern of rooms formed through the centuries.

Dad was staying with my sister in South Africa at the time and when he came home he too seemed glad to find everything complete and finished, but said he wished to see Mr Haldane, and I hoped that he had come round to welcoming the improvements at last.

Mr Haldane duly arrived and met Dad and his wheelchair in the large panelled hall.

"I think what you have done is atrocious!" roared Dad, "and you should be ashamed of yourself!"

What a shock! I dived into the drinks cupboard for much needed brandy and not only for Mr Haldane! He was indeed badly shaken, but today we can both smile, remembering.

I always knew that Dad wanted to retain the 1921 plans, but I also knew they didn't do justice to the beautiful building. It was he who had let the place relapse into such disrepair and I could afford to update only once. I had shown him the plans before the work commenced and he had said nothing. Whenever Dad was really 'cornered up' he always remained silent, refusing to comment.

I tried again. "If Dad, for some reason you had gone back to live in Grandpa's house, High Leas, would you not have wished to change some things around?" a question which not unnaturally angered him, being unable to deny the charge, and met again with stony silence.

My sisters were both critical and angry. They thought I was too hard on Dad; there was even a letter muttering about the 'invasion of storm troopers', which of course he showed me.

Another to my face was,

"Oh I suppose it's alright if you like all that white paint!" That one really hurt.

They thought I should have spent my money on central heating and repairs and kept the 1920's plan, which is what Dad wanted, but they didn't have to live here, and never considered how difficult it would have been for my children, grandchildren and our friends to stay, when Dad's desk, which he used constantly, was in the middle of the one small sitting-room.

Our nursery had become the dining-room when Dad altered the original into his billiard room. The rest of the downstairs area was all utilities. There would have been nowhere for me to entertain friends and family and nowhere for children to sit or play, except in the kitchen.

In succeeding years, Dad came to enjoy the hall with its excellent log burner warming the whole room. He loved to have a men's bridge four, and I rustled up some old boys, bridge players, from near where I had lived, and they all got on like a house on fire.

I had some trouble with their wives who thought they should be invited too! But the day was as special for me as it was for him, because I could work in the garden for hours with a clear conscience, knowing that he was as happy as myself, so I'm afraid I ignored the female protests.

I made old fashioned teas for Dad's bridge players, with home made teacakes, scones and small savoury sandwiches and a cake. The three guests arrived at two, already in good humour having lunched at the 'Drum and Monkey,' an excellent fish restaurant in Harrogate, and they usually stayed till six and had a whiskey before departure.

I felt sorry for the very nice Conservative agent for the Thirsk area, who made up the 'fourth' player and whom I hadn't met before, but came to like immensely. My old boys insisted he must drive them, saying they were too elderly and, being the man he was, I am sure he resisted the temptation of wine with lunch and certainly refused Dad's whiskey at the end of the day.

He was very good to me and between us we managed to save one of the 'lads' from a crashing fall when he entered through the front door, having perhaps, over imbibed at lunch!

All Dad's friends were amazed by the improvements in the house. They said Low Hall had been the coldest, darkest house in Yorkshire, its transformation was wonderful. They even said so to Dad, but only once.

"I think it's atrocious!" he repeated and any further conversation on the subject dried up after that.

I must add here that both Dad and Mummy were wonderfully generous about my levelling the garden. It had 'gone back', even the apple trees near the house had died, so I set about redesigning it from scratch and this involved my parents being surrounded by workmen, noise and pretty much a ploughed field for over a year, and they never complained…not once.

Dad had never taken much interest in the garden before— he considered it to be Mother's department, and she and Bert had made it very pretty. It was the grass tennis court, so near, and to one side of the house, that obstructed any hope of a pleasing balance, so I took it out.

As time continued Dad became fascinated by all the new

colour and development of a little pond garden. He often walked round and wanted his friends to see it too. One day he told Dee he was very upset due to my having cut down the flowers outside his bedroom window. He loved the colour and not all of them had quite died. It was fun to reassure and explain that they would flower again in the autumn, due to the present pruning, so he could look forward to enjoy a second flowering of the campanula lactiflora in August or September.

* * *

To return to 1929, we children all had nicknames. Dorothy, the eldest, was 'Dodo' but later became Dee; Elizabeth, two years younger, was Buffin; Phil, our brother, who came next, was Puyug (Pussy Rug) due to a fur rug he loved to wrap round himself. Almost inevitably my name Pamela was shortened to Pamjam.

Dee was seven when I was born, and both she and Buffin had started school. I loved them but for me they belonged in a different world from Phil and myself. He was three years older than me, and I suspect he had as much fun with them as with myself, but at the time I firmly believed he was all mine.

Thinking of this early childhood, I picture the blue-green linoleum of our rooms where there were little mats beside each bed. When Dad was at home, on Sunday mornings, I woke to his laughter, and before I knew it he had me by the ankle, and I was flying, then spinning across the cold polished floor. He did it expertly, in no way roughly, it never hurt, and I expect the boys had the same treatment. I squeaked with laughter too but felt the game was more fun for him than for me, but it never occurred to me to protest.

As well as caring for us children so well, Mother organised

the household round what pleased her husband. Alice our cook learnt to employ onions in recipes just enough to improve flavour without Dad knowing they were there. Mother learned to make masses of marmalade using his family recipe, and no other kind would do. Meals were presented at the times that suited him and always to his taste, in fact she spoiled him rotten. He was the king in his castle. I have a distant memory of him being served with a green crispy apple, peeled and sliced on a white plate in bed before breakfast, but think that must have occurred only at weekends.

We children grew up understanding that Dad was the most important person in our lives. Whatever we might be doing, Mummy saw that we would be waiting around to welcome his home-coming each evening. Dad, I rather think, took this for granted but he never made a big fuss of us; hugs and kisses weren't the fashion in my childhood. Be that as it may I never doubted that he loved us.

I wonder now whether Dad's long life was permanently shadowed by the heroic death of his elder brother Phil whom he had worshipped. If he was trying to emulate Phil's extraordinary courage, he succeeded. Dad was one of the bravest people I have known, but he was also modest and never thought he was anything out of the ordinary.

In her speech at his funeral Buffin said that she believed Dad was so grateful to be alive at all, after his appalling war experience, he determined he would never waste another minute of his life, and I don't think he did.

His joy and enthusiasm for the two sports he loved, Yorkshire hunting and salmon fishing in the Highlands, continued until he was in his late seventies.

I jumped too far ahead and return to our early childhood.

Our large, downstairs nursery had French windows, which would, in previous times, have been the main entrance to the house, but now fronted on to flower borders and lawns, leading to Mother's little rose garden, quartered round an old stone bird-bath, each bed edged with Mrs Sinkin's pinks.

There was an overgrown lilac growing close by, and it, with roses and pinks, created a strong heady mixture of scent in those far off summers. The nursery had window-seats under high mullions in which Mother kept her sewing machine, materials and wools. A fine seamstress, she made all the house curtains, choosing pretty linen chintz, and she also sewed or knitted many of our clothes.

Phil was my hero in those first years and I can see myself now, racing downstairs, the Monkey family in my arms, and he, waiting for us, in front of the white painted toy cupboard, that Grandpa's joiner, Sam Ingham had made large, good and solid, like the man himself.

Phil's birthday present had arrived last night, when the Monkey Family was already in bed, and I knew they would be longing to see it. Mr and Mrs Monkey were white with smiley, brown velvet faces and silky fur on their very long tails, the twins were just like them but small and woolly, and the family and I were inseparable at the time.

We tucked ourselves in beside Phil, as he lifted the large red box from a shelf in the cupboard

"Ready?" he said, and I nodded. He opened the lid. We all gazed at the beautiful red Hornby engine in her slot, surrounded by her tender and trucks, and could hardly believe our eyes.

Phil let me help to lay out the aluminium rails, and explained they must fit together exactly, so they would lie firm and flat on the floor and not lift up as some seemed to want to do. The Monkey family sat leaning their backs against the cupboard door and watched our every move.

Dee and Buffin were rearranging things in their doll's house, and came over to look. It was decided that the doll's house family wished to move house, so we loaded the tiny furniture into the trucks. Phil wound up the engine with a big silver key, and she obligingly pulled her load expertly, right across to the other side of the nursery.

Phil was given more engines in later years. There was a larger and more powerful green one, that had beautiful coffee-brown Pulman coaches trimmed with gold, one of which was a diner, with little tables set out for tea inside; but the engine had an extra set of wheels, which made it cumbersome and it was always falling off the rails going round corners. However exotic, none gave us the same thrill as the first red engine.

In the middle of the nursery there was a pedestal table which we discovered was hinged, so we turned over the top to make a slide, and used the window-seat cushions to soften our landing. Remembering the high excitement of tearing round, one after the other, and scrambling up a chair to get back to the top, is now almost impossible to believe. I found the old table in a barn a few years ago and it was no size at all!

More daring, for Phil and myself, was our sliding down the banister rail of the stairs which on one side had a sharp, deep fall to the shadowed hall below, and an unforgiving square oak post at the bottom if one went too fast.

Another occasion finds Phil and me under the same table, industriously filing cardboard. It is slow work, but we don't need much. We are making tobacco and Phil has cigarette papers and knows how to roll them. He runs the tip of his tongue expertly along the edge of the paper, just as Charlie does on the farm.

We slip from the house and run across the Blown Tree Pasture, climb the style and crawl down the bank above the river. It is very steep, too steep to walk.

"Take care!" he says, but I am safe as houses.

Phil has found what he calls a cave, but it is not exactly a cave, it is a flat rock round which has grown a great stunted oak. The lowest branches lead out horizontally, like giant arms, and then circle back over the water, so we are completely hidden in the foliage.

We sit on the rock, our legs dangling over a twenty-foot drop to the deep pool below, and light up. We find our cigarettes delicious.

Walking back from the river, Phil pauses, feeling for the strong mints needed in case Mother smells our breath. Out of his pocket comes a penknife and some string, and then, with the mints, two or three halfpennies.

At that moment, we hear the train, revving up its puff, climbing the hill this side of Darley, so we scamper across to the railway line and Phil squeezes through the fence and places the coins on a rail.

He comes back, just in time and I grab his hand as the train roars past, immediately above us. How lucky! One of the coins has flattened into an almost perfect round, so Phil runs down to the village, where Ernest Abbott has his shop with a chocolate slot-machine outside.

I wait where I am. You have to pass through Proctor's farm on the way, and old Grannie Proctor is always chalking her front door step and yells at us just like a banshee.

She frightens Dee and Buffin so much, they walk up the

farm lane right to the road, rather than risk passing through Proctor's. But nothing frightens Phil, he doesn't give a hoot for old Grannie P., and when he comes back we share the penny bar, munching as we go home.

Before our cousin Peter came to live with us, Phil and I shared a small, square room at the back of the house. Facing north, it got no sun but had a magnificent unspoilt view of the Dale. Through the lacework of three tremendous ash trees we could see the roofs of the village, beyond which the land rose with its criss cross pattern of dry stone walls, up and up to a great dome of sky. Under the lip of the moors we could just make out stone farmhouses and barns looking back down on us from some thousand feet above the valley floor.

When our cousin Peter came to live with us, we tried to think of a good name for him, but he beat us to it.

"I am 'The Greater Gambini!!'" he intoned dramatically, and the name stuck.

He had been ill with malaria and was smaller than Phil and six months younger. It wasn't long before we thought of him as another brother. He was always fun and pulled the most terrible faces to make me laugh; he was good at tennis too. Phil had to work hard to beat him on the court, and sometimes didn't manage it. Gambini could use either hand equally well and never had to learn how to do backhand.

Phil and I introduced him to our river cave and he tried out our cigarettes, swore they were delicious, turned green and was violently sick; it happened every time but never deterred him from smoking them! I moved in with my sisters when Gambini arrived and slept in a large room facing south over the garden. Mummy gave us three brand-new, blue, two foot six wide divans with interior springs, but even they failed to compensate for my loss of Phil's company. I was astonished and affronted by Dee's fury when she found me borrowing her toothbrush. Phil and I had always shared everything, even toffees sometimes.

In memory, summers were always sunny and warm, and we children often lazed on the lower lawn under the dappled shade of two old Keswick Apple trees, while our elders disported themselves on the grass court above and Annie Busfield, our maid, brought tea out for everyone.

Mr Cardale, the nice plumpish vicar from Hartwith, and a great friend of our parents, was playing one day, and threw himself into one of those simple deck chairs which consist of a length of canvas slung over a light wooden frame, and he went straight through. He was stuck fast and we couldn't release him, and the more he laughed the fatter he got. In the end we had to turn him over on to his knees and pull what was left of the chair from him that way.

In those days the front of the house was covered with thick Virginia creeper and we girls woke in early summer to the sounds of much busy fluttering and rustling of hundreds of sparrows nesting round our bedroom windows, and one year a starling, perched on the roof of the barn, greeted the dawn with a beautiful fluted whistle, which made one dream of a stream pouring down a distant waterfall.

Sparrows are the gypsies of the bird world, and careless little creatures. Many chicks fell out of the overloaded nests and I found their naked little bodies on the path below, and gave each a formal burial with flowers until the numbers defeated me.

Inevitably I had to go to bed first, and dear Mrs Walsh, our nannie, drew the curtains. Hot sunshine shone through them in squares like the windows and I could hear shouts and laughter from the tennis court below. Then the unmistakable thud of tennis ball on grass and best of all a wild shot clonks against the mullions. I can't sleep, I am out of bed, peeping through the curtains, almost joining in the scene below.

Mrs Walsh was Roman Catholic and must have confessed to the local priest that she had run away from her husband who had horribly abused her. Few country priests would have had the courage to protect her secret in those days, and certainly ours did not. He harried and frightened her persistently until she finally gave in and returned to the husband.

This haunted Mother for the rest of her life. She had begged Mrs Walsh to stay, made her promise to keep in touch, but never a word came back. I think for some time Mother hoped she might reappear because she didn't engage another nannie. Instead, Dorothy Houseman, a very dear daughter of a local farmer, came in on a daily basis to help with me for a year or two.

When Phil and Peter started school I had the farm to myself, and was not so adventurous, but dear Bert our gardener/handyman, became an even closer friend and we worked together in the garden and I 'helped' him feed the hens which were housed in wooden huts scattered round the farm. Both water and feed had to be carried to them, and one evening when I was collecting eggs from the hut near our Dutch barn, I put my hand in the nesting-box to find a live rat rather than an egg. He was as surprised as myself and shot out over my shoulder!

I rode in the heavy, wooden feed bin that ran on a little railway in front of the cows tied in the mistal. Don pushed it along as he rhythmically shovelled out the exact amount of feed each animal required.

Often I climbed a ladder to the hay lofts where farm cats lived and nested. I searched for kittens and usually found some, the mother curled round them, proudly welcoming me with a lifted paw to let me see her babies. But one had to be careful: the now grown-up kittens from Darley Mill continued to be wild and scratchy, and I could never persuade them to become friends.

Mummy and I had walked on the river path down to the mill one lovely summer's day when Mr Skaife said he had some spare kittens. All our farm cats had died from 'cat flu' and it was vital to find replacements immediately. Rats and mice caused terrible loss in cattle feeds if the farm had no cats, there being no such thing as rat poison in those days. We heard the deep rumbling of Mr Skaife's mill long before we reached it, and when we entered the vast, shadowed interior, we felt underfoot the vibration and shudder of its great wheel turning the water, round and round. Laddered steps led us up from one level to the next, and we saw the men tipping the grain down a central hole in the floors, polished like silk from two hundred years of heavy sacks being pulled across them .

Mr Skaife, himself, was a thin, kind man, whose overalls were stiff and cracked, caked with dry flour from the grain. He wore thick, round-rimmed glasses, and they, like his face and hair, were covered in white dust.

We found the kittens, fast asleep in a heap of tabby velvet in a little loft and Mr Skaife picked them up gingerly amid loud squeaks, hissing and scratchy paws, then popped them swiftly into the basket Mother had brought, and she tucked them round with a blue chequered tea towel, so they couldn't escape. He carried the basket down for her, saying,

"The mother's as wild as on the day she arrived, a feral cat we've never been able to tame, but these kits will do your job, she's the best ratter we've had in the mill."

We thanked him, and I remember him standing there quietly watching us across the road, such a kind man. All the way home we made up names for the kits and I found Don was waiting for me. He showed me a little nest of hay he'd made for the kittens near two cracked saucers in the stall next to our house cow. He said he would leave a jug of milk for them every morning, but I must bring scraps from the house to feed them, and it became my first job on the farm.

We relied on Ernest Abbott's shop in the village for all necessities. A range of foods was laid out on a counter downstairs, hams hung from the ceiling, and Mrs Abbott sold overalls and gumboots and other basic clothes and sewing things upstairs, in the cold room above. I remember Phil and I buying cheese one day when Ernest couldn't find a wire to cut it. Phil picked up a piece of binder twine from the floor and said,

"Will this do, Ernest?" and without a thought Ernest said it was just the job. No Health and Safety in those days, but we never came to any harm!

Ernest made deliveries in his van every week, and sometimes I popped in beside him and went on his round. The occasion I remember, was to West End and I helped him to carry some boxes across a little iron bridge over a stream, on the other side of which lived Mrs Waite.

Mrs Waite had a wooden leg and was a great friend of Ernest's. They put me in the parlour while they swopped local news over a mug of tea.

The parlour was the most fascinating place I'd ever been in. Mrs Waite collected clocks of every kind, large and small and they ticked busily in solid rows filling every space on all four of the parlour walls. It was the first time I had seen a cuckoo clock, and with luck the hour would change while I was there. The volume and clatter of chimes and striking was almost frightening and, best of all, the little bird shot out from behind his door and cucked!

Poor West End village and surrounding farms now lie under the compensation reservoir needed by the wider development of Leeds and Bradford. In droughty summers in a reservoir nearby, the tower of the church emerges above the water and is a reminder of how dreadful it must have been for the people to lose their homes, and even worse for the farmers who lost not only their houses but also their land, their livelihood, inheritance and jobs. Whatever the compensation, nothing can ever have matched such personal tragedies.

In early November, we carefully picked out our turnips to make into lanterns for Bonfire Night. I wasn't yet trusted to use a knife, and scooping out a turnip with a kitchen spoon is very hard work!

It took days to convert all our turnips into beautiful lanterns with carved grinning faces. Mummy cut off the tops first and then knifed in a hole to act as a chimney. The more we scraped the better the result. When ready to insert the candles and experiment in lighting them, a thin-skinned lantern glowed all over. We used red tissue paper for mouths and blue, if we could get it, for eyes. The better made lanterns sported teeth in an otherwise toothless grin.

Whatever the weather, on the Saturday evening nearest to November the 5th we filed out of the house into the dark, each carrying his lantern on a loop of string and walked in crocodile to a little area of semi-woodland. We hung the lanterns on the low branch of an old alder tree, and they looked very cheerful bobbing up and down, grinning back at us.

Dad lit the wonderful bonfire that the men had built from rubbish, mostly timber, collected through the past year, and it always started first time, with a great whoosh of flame straight up into the dark sky. We danced round waving our sparklers, and then there were a few fireworks and Catherine wheels before one last, really dramatic rocket, that flew twice as high as the others and released drifting bubbles of colour that floated slowly earthward before disappearing.

One year a spent rocket shot down poor Buffin's gumboot, and she bore the small scar of a very painful burn for the rest of her days.

Remembering those parties brings back the delicious smell of hot turnip cooking in the flame of the lanterns as we sallied forth, and then the fun we had next day when we returned, each armed with a large potato, taken from the 'farm pie'. Dee was in charge of the packet of butter, and off we went, back to last night's fire, to roast the potatoes in its still hot ashes. They might have been made in heaven, all crispy outside and hot and soft within, eaten with our fingers. No food today can compare with the wonderful taste of those old spuds.

For years we children believed that it was a hare that brought the chocolate eggs for which we searched in the garden on Easter Sunday, but the theory did not sit comfortably when we had watched, spellbound, wild March hares boxing in the river fields below the Hall. We must have pestered our parents with questions because Dad promised he would wake us early the following Easter so that we could see the Hare.

When the day came round, our parents put much thought into the event, and hid the eggs in the garden very early,

Mother used the old vicuna rug from the back of the sitting-room sofa to wrap round herself and slipped through a gate into the field just beyond the garden and hopped about here and there, pretending to nibble grass.

Dad woke us and with noses pressed against the mullions, we watched a very realistic-looking hare in the field and were entranced until there was a wild, rough shout from the farmyard above. It was Don, who had always believed Low Hall to be haunted.

"Jack, Jack! Fetch a pitch fork from the barn and chase that apparition out of the field!" he yelled.

Jack leapt the wall into the meadow in no time, and we girls wept with terror as we saw him gaining on the lovely hare, his pitch fork poised at the ready. The hare appeared to be unaware of its danger, which made it all the more scary.

Thankfully she slipped over the low wall into the woods on the farther end of the field, just before Jack caught up with her, and when he came home he told us that he saw no sign of her in the woods, our hare had completely vanished when he looked over the wall.

Another Easter Sunday we looked out and saw a life-size, chocolate Scottie with large yellow bow on the lawn, but our very alive cairn terrier, Corrie, had found him first!

These happy years slipped by in no time and when I was five I joined my sisters at Belmont and started off in the kindergarten; the boys were at Grosvenor House, both schools in Harrogate.

Due to the severity of weather that winter, Ripley Lake froze solid and the Ingilbys of Ripley Castle kindly opened the Park so everyone could skate. Mummy collected us from school at half past three, having packed our skates in the car, and we joined friends and played ice hockey with Dad's old golf clubs, using a discarded polo chuck that we had collected.

Polo teams had matches on the Stray in Harrogate every summer in those days and we often watched. The boys collected broken sticks as well as chucks and played bicycle polo in the fields at home, much to the detriment of spokes.

Dee and Buffin must have been given skating boots, as I found two pairs in a barn a few years ago, but the boys and I had screw-on skates, always coming loose and falling off.

Being the youngest and wobbly, I was usually goalie, but no one minded if I drifted off on my own now and then, and I remember one occasion when I had noticed an old black oak, climbing against a glorious, early sunset sky. As I skated towards it, a skein of low-flying Canada Geese swooshed overhead, and I followed their flight with my eyes, leaning back till I fell flat, cracking my head on the ice. A bit stunned but otherwise unhurt, I was glad none of the family noticed my idotic fall, it was not a moment for being teased. I slowly got upright again and heard Mummy calling from the bank.

"Time to go home!" And there she was, holding a thermos of boiling Heinz tomato soup. She helped me off with my skates, and I warmed chilled hands round the mug, I felt the soup slip down, down into my tummy, and it was, perhaps the best moment of the day.

When I was seven, Dee and Buffin left home to board at Queen Anne's, a girls' school in Caversham, and the boys became weekly boarders instead of dayboys at Grosvenor House. I left Belmont and had the luck to go to Miss Walker's school in Ripon as a weekly boarder too.

Miss Walker's School

DRIVE OVER THE RIVER bridge today, and the house is still there, the first in a long Victorian Crescent facing back across the river to the town. It was No.1 Yore Bank . . . now Ure Bank, for some reason. But the railway has gone. Neither its bridge nor the small garage beneath it, where Nancy kept her car, remain; all that has become an enormous roundabout.

There is time, so I turn and enter the lane with Mr Phillip's river fields on my left and pause. On my right is the remembered small, wrought-iron gate and steps leading up to the front porch. There too is the oddly shaped garden with a high walled point at one end, created by the back lane which led to the old bobbin mill we boarders used to visit.

There as well is the large, lead-lined balcony above the bay windows of what once was the beautiful drawing-room. Miss C. Walker was a great believer in the benefits of fresh air, and on fine mornings she would open the schoolroom's high, wide windows on the first floor for us children to step on to the balcony and breathe deep breaths. We competed to see who could hold out the longest, and ended up with many explosive giggles.

Later, half way through morning lessons we ran out into the garden for a ten minute break, and bobbed up and down trying to emulate Miss C.'s various and vigorous exercises. Clear as crystal, I see her nut brown, highly polished shoes with narrow diagonal strap across elegant ankles, and they are leaping . . . out in! in out! And I am in the front of the little queue of children facing her on the narrow box-lined path, trying to keep in time, and the scent of philadelphus and old-fashioned roses, lavender and pinks is all round us.

Now, all that has gone. The untidy but lovely garden has been ripped out and layered into three severe levels of plain cut lawn, some hideous, brightly painted apparatus at the top —and it hurts. Foolishly I had hoped something more of the happy childhood place might still remain.

I turn the car and continue on my way, but the visit has revived old memories and I can think of little else.

I was seven when I went to weekly board at Miss Walker's in 1936, and it was an old dames' school that catered for some sixteen children. Its ethos was very much *The Wind in the Willows*, *The Secret Garden*, 'Saki', Rudyard Kipling's poetry; and its influence had a strong effect on us all.

The half-hour lessons were hard work but always interesting. We were highly disciplined but never aware of it. Everyone tried their best, was rewarded accordingly and enjoyed it. Several amongst us were to become lifelong friends.

We learned to read with a book, *Reading without Tears*, which started with a picture of a cat (or dog) at the top of a column of rhyming words. Below each column were words that sounded the same but were spelt differently which we called exceptions, and learned by heart. Then there were a few lines of story about the cat which contained most of the words in the column, and it imbued us with a facility for both reading and accurate spelling.

Joined up writing came in a copy book with double lines. Every curve had to be drawn so the letter just touched the top or bottom of the trams, and letters with legs must protrude above and below the lines at exactly the same length.

We learnt many things by heart. Tables up to twelve times nineteen; the dates and names of all the Kings and Queens; our capital cities, their county and river. We learned both psalms and poetry by heart too and were awarded stars when we managed to recite them perfectly.

There was a board by the mantelpiece to stick the gold stars, and next to it another for order marks, and on one memorable occasion a red conduct mark, when the doctor's daughter Jean tapped someone with her ruler.

Maths were taught on slates, and afforded one of the few distractions to concentration when someone managed to screech his lead pencil across the surface, which set everyone's teeth on edge!

There were two Miss Walker sisters: Fran, the elder, a semi-invalid and somewhat retiring, and Christine (Miss C.) who was the inspiration and heart of the place. Their niece Nancy ran the household with the help of Mary the maid, who bicycled from the other side of town every day to polish and clean everything in sight.

Strangely, the four adults adopted exactly the same hairstyle. They plaited their hair into two coils that were pinned each side of the head, creating a 'bang' behind the ear. Miss C.'s was faded copper, Miss F.'s soft grey, Nancy's a rich brown, and Mary's jet black, and she wore black woollen stockings, shiny black shoes, black dresses, and her large black eyes sparkled through thick, black-rimmed spectacles under heavy brows. Her aprons and headgear were starched white and crunchy, but the severity of her appearance was totally negated by a wide and beaming smile. Almost inevitably, her heavy sit-up-and-beg bicycle was as black and solid as the Ace of Spades.

Mr Phillips, who farmed the land between the Terrace and the river, gave us permission to use his field for games, and he appeared at the kitchen door every morning with a large can of still warm milk, some of which Nancy poured into five glasses, before they were carried down to the cellar.

When they reappeared on a tray in the evening, with a digestive biscuit, like a lid on top of each glass, there was a half inch layer of rich cream below, and we boarders had competitions for who could create the biggest cream moustache, and never again has milk tasted so good.

Another small ritual remains a mystery to this day. At each end of the schoolroom mantelpiece stood a decorative blue and white china mug, and every morning senna pods in each were steeping and steaming in newly boiled water and remained in position all day. We always wondered why they were placed in the schoolroom rather than all the other more likely places in the house, but we never found out.

I was one of five boarders. We three girls slept on the top floor of the house which vibrated and shook every night when the Express from London to Edinburgh shot through Ripon Station, just behind the house. Its speed was such that the old sash windows in our bedroom clattered and chattered too, as though they were speeding it on. Bill and Peter, the boy boarders, had a bedroom on the first floor opposite the schoolroom.

When the day children went home, Nancy would take us boarders for nature walks . . . naming wild flowers was an important part of our curriculum, and whoever found the first of its kind and brought a specimen to school, had their name and that of the flower, with its date, written up on a board.

Sometimes Nancy drove us further afield in her old black Morris which was also used for taking us to the Town Hall for dancing classes with Miss Hyde on Thursdays. The car was Nancy's pride and joy, and she kept it with the nice man who had his garage under the railway bridge close by.

I remember us all standing in the middle of Sharow Lane one Autumn, trying to catch falling beech leaves, not a car in sight. The leaves dipped this way and that as they sailed downwards and were very difficult to get hold of, but Nancy said if we achieved twelve, we would have twelve happy months next year.

On cold wintry afternoons we followed a path from the lane that led through a wood of colossal old beeches and Dog's Mercury flowered its dull fusty flowers at their dry earthy roots in early Spring.

In summer we walked further and found the wood opened out on to low river meadows, where the boys and I would paddle barefoot in squelchy mud, building harbours for imaginary boats, and I see Nancy sitting on a little knoll of grass above us, her straw hat yellow in mellow sunshine, a picnic basket beside her waiting for teatime.

Bill and Peter were my best friends. Bill was the 'naughty' boy in school, an expert at 'screeching' his slate pencil in Maths lessons, and usually festooned with bandages round his thin little knees and the rough skin on his hands. He suffered from eczema and asthma, but managed to ignore both, and was always full of adventurous ideas. Peter was quiet and thoughtful and spoke slowly in a dreamy sort of way and he fitted perfectly into my life. I never doubted we would marry one day.

In the large, drawing-room on the ground floor there was always a fire, because Miss F. felt the cold. She sat in one of the comfortable armchairs with a soft woollen shawl about her shoulders and there were three or four child-sized tables and chairs placed round her for the youngest children, to whom she introduced the three 'Rs.'

Birthdays were celebrated, and usually all the children were invited to a party held in one's home. Mother found someone to make sixteen little boats for my party one year, and she sewed miniature sacks of corn, doll's house size barrels and other cargoes which had to be loaded at several "ports" down one of the farm's streams. The party was a great success but Henry's parties were always the most interesting. His mother Lady Doris Vyner owned Fountains Abbey in those days, and Henry's birthday was in the summer like mine, and we had wonderful treasure hunts all through the ruins with excellent cream teas in the beautiful seventeenth-century Hall just within its gates.

Henry's Christmas party was in the family's Yorkshire home Studley Royal, a magnificent Georgian house near Fountains Abbey, and I remember standing in my pink party frock, gazing at the vast, elegant staircase in the inner hall when I was supposed to be having tea in the dining-room with everyone else. The staircase was divided; each side curved upward to meet on the mezzanine, then continued broad and shallow to the next floor, which was rounded and oval, all decked with classical wrought-iron balustrade. High, high above, there glimmered a roundel of glass and how I longed to see what else was up there! I determined to live in a house with just such a gracious stairway when I grew up.

We were driving home from one of Henry's Christmas parties when there had been an early fall of snow, and Mummy and I got stuck in drifts on Brimham Rocks. It was dark and the wind had driven the snow into great drifts. I had only a light coat over the party dress and was wearing my dancing shoes, so Mummy left me in the car and went off to search for help.

The car was stone cold and pitch black and, left alone, I was seriously frightened and nearly frozen. I thought my mother might get lost and never come back, a haunting possibility, but not for long. She had the luck to meet a snowplough almost immediately and back she came in the driver's cab where I soon joined her. He drove us to the main road and dropped us off at an inn. I remember the glorious warmth of the kitchen fire and being given hot milk laced with golden syrup, and hope that Mummy was revived with something stronger.

In my second year, 1939, war broke out, and I returned to school with my gas-mask and brand new siren suit, a warm and cuddly 'all-in-one' job with feet. There followed many air raid warnings, mostly false alarums, due to the proximity of Dishforth aerodrome, always at night and sometimes twice in a night.

We woke to the terrifying wail of sirens, shot out of bed and raced down three staircases into the cellar. Once there we curled up with rugs and slept again, feeling safe and secure amidst delicious smells of onions and herbs and apples stored round us. It was only the sirens that were frightening.

I stayed at Miss Walker's for five years, ending up as head-girl, and in spite of the war we children lived in a blissful bubble of security. We were taught high standards and self-respect; we were capable of taking on responsibilities as we grew older and were aware of living in difficult, even fearful times, but neither fear nor anxiety was allowed to penetrate into our school life.

Due to Ripon being a base for the Royal Engineers, the town became very full with new people at the beginning of the war. The camp expanded and Army families followed. The Miss Walkers engaged another teacher as more and more children arrived and one small girl told me about the odd person who lived in the flat below them.

"She wears wigs," she announced, "and sometimes looks like a man!"

Either one of us told Miss C. or she overheard the conversation and reported the story to the Military Police. She took me on one side the next day and told me I must never ever repeat the story. The strange lady was in fact a German spy and under surveillance. The Military Police were hoping she might lead them to her contacts.

Home that weekend I could not resist telling the boys that I had a Military Secret and of course they tried and tried to get it out of me. The questioning and pleas continued non-stop through the weekend and I found it difficult not to split—it was only the thought of letting down Miss C. that kept me going. I complained to Mummy, asked her to stop the boys teasing me, but she was on their side for once and said I should have thought about that before mentioning the secret! Eventually we all forgot about it, and I never spoke of it to anyone for years and years.

Remembering as I drive on, Miss C. Walker comes alive in my mind. Spry and sweet and much loved. I can't thank her enough for giving me such a good start in life. Nancy too, so small and rounded and jolly, remained a friend for years. She loved us children and always slipped upstairs to tuck us in and say Goodnight.

In the time of Phil

PHIL was not so fortunate. When he sat for his Common Entrance for Loretto, a school in Musselburgh, my parents learned that his standard of work was well below that expected, and they arranged for a Cambridge student to give him extra tuition throughout the holidays.

Peter Browning's family lived in Seaford, Sussex, and he was one of three brothers. Their father, a parson, had died young and their mother, whom we came to know well in future years, was a tall, indomitable widow, with a wooden leg.

Peter came into our lives, all six foot of him, with startling, blue eyes set under short, curly dark hair, and an engaging smile that revealed perfect and very white teeth.

Everyone liked him immediately, and after working with Phil in the mornings he joined in with whatever was happening. There was a very bad winter that year, and Peter's presence added verve to our sledging races down the farm lane. Phil would captain one and Peter the other in neck and neck competition. It was almost inevitable that seventeen year-old Dee would fall in love with Peter, and he with her.

Being a weekly boarder at Miss Walker's, and all of us older, we played as a family much more in the holidays, and one Easter we built a house in the woods by a little stream. Using larch poles, we dug them in, upright, to create the walls, and Buffin insisted the house must have a window which somewhat complicated the simple structure. Much more serious were the draughts. We couldn't pitch the poles close enough, and someone came up with the idea of weaving heather between them.

It must have been on a Sunday that we took Jerry, the oldest carthorse, up to the moors to pull heather, as there was no one around to help. Phil knew how to harness Jerry but we couldn't lift the heavy collar over his head. Phil had to climb up and stand in his waist-high iron trough and we passed the collar up to him. I remember he had to turn it round as it slid down the horse's neck to fit it snug against his old shoulders.

Pulling heather took all day and was harder work than expected, but we took a picnic with us, and in the end the cart was full. How lovely it was, tired out and happy, lying in the honey-scented heather, half asleep, and hearing the chink of Jerry's metal shoes ring out rhythmically against the road, going home.

We finished the house on the last day of the Easter holidays, and Mum and Dad joined us for a celebratory supper, our fireplace in the stump of a fallen beech. Bacon, eggs and sausages, cooked in a frying pan over the dying embers, never tasted better.

We had ideas of planting a woodland garden round the house, but I don't remember using the place again; the fun had been in the building. However I found some daffodils flowering on the bank a year or two back, so we must have planted a few bulbs.

The stream that runs past where our tree house used to be continues down to the railway, where a tunnel had had to be built to give the train passage over it. It exemplifies the best of Victorian building, made of cut stone and perfectly circular, a small work of art.

We found that we could enter it without getting wet if we placed our feet against its rounded sides just above water level, and soon discovered there was a splendid echo.

The greatest excitement however, was when the train ran over it. There was terrific vibration and noise as it approached, and everything seemed to rock! When it was immediately overhead hot smoke and steam poured into the tunnel, so we couldn't see, and someone usually lost their balance and fell into the stream.

We often took our friends there to share the experience. Mummy was always having to find spare socks and shorts to be worn while the wet clothes were hung out on the drying-green outside the kitchen.

Time was moving irrevocably towards the Second World War. Dee enjoyed Queen Anne's and being at boarding school, but poor Buffin never settled. I don't think she told anyone, not even Mother, but years later she confessed to having been terribly homesick and that Dee hadn't seemed to understand.

For her, the war turned out to be a temporary blessing. The Roman Catholic convent in Harrogate agreed to squeeze her in to its school, and for the next two years, prior to attending Atholl Crescent's Domestic Science Course, when she was seventeen, Buffin learned fast, made lifelong friends and excelled in most subjects, not least Lacrosse.

In another very severe winter, Bert had made two large sledges for us all. They weighed like lead and went very fast, each one large enough to carry three or four people. Phil found an old cocoa tin and punched holes in the lid and bottom, installed a roll of corrugated paper and lit it before take off. I thought it marvellous and always tried to be on his sledge, and see the 'exhaust' smoke whirling behind us!

The farm lane was so deep in drifts that the carthorses went up by the fields and came down pulling the wooden snowplough behind them. Their hooves roughed up the snow in the middle of the lane, but left two solid flat paths each side, perfect for us to race the sledges.

Peter Browning more than entered the excitement of racing and added to the fun. On a good day we shot the half mile run without a break, and the very steep approach at the end was a real hazard, it being a thick-cut holly hedge just above the Hall.

With Bert's help, Phil and Gambini constructed two trollies made from perambulator wheels so we could continue to race in the Easter holidays, and again it was the greatest fun, not quite as fast, but good enough for the excitement of a neck and neck finish.

In memory, there were always ponies at home, and Buffin and Phil enjoyed the Bramham Moor pony-club camps. Dee never rode after a fall when she broke her arm, and I was too young to attend the camps.

Dad always loved horses and had been a good horseman. In the obituaries after Uncle Phil's death, someone remarked that he had been an outstanding horseman, and I believe Dad had been the same, but now, due to the wound that almost destroyed one knee, he had no grip and just stayed on top somehow, but still wanted me to learn.

I must have been seven or eight years old when Phil and I bicycled to Ripley where Mr Beaumont kept a riding stable and gave lessons. I liked my pony but had little idea of how to manage him, so he shot straight under the low branches of a tree, and I was swept from the saddle and landed on my back in the field. Quite unhurt, I thought the accident very funny, lying there and gazing up into the blue sky. But Mr Beaumont was simply furious. I must have given him the fright of his life, as I could easily have been killed. Certainly this taught me never to ride under trees again, and the lesson proceeded without further excitement.

Bicycling home, Phil noticed a low lorry, loaded with hay, was climbing up the steep of Bedlam Bank, and suggested we hang on behind and got pulled up. I touched the back of the lorry but could not bring myself to do it. I was filled with terror, visualizing the load slipping off the cart and coming down on top of us. At the same time I knew it would not and was heartily ashamed of my panic, but unable to control it. It must have been irritating for Phil, but he said nothing. Without a word he placed his hand on the flat of my back and pushed me up the long hill himself. I still feel the warmth of his hand today, and the memory brings tears.

One day Dad said I must ride with him, and my pony Spider was a stubborn little person, who nearly always got her own way. Entering some woodland, Dad jumped across a small stream and told me to follow.

"Spider can jump it easily," he said.

"Of course" I replied, "but I can't make her."

"Well give it a try!"

We trotted smartly to the stream where she instantly stopped dead and put her nose down to drink. I shot down her neck and landed head first in the stream. Dad laughed till he ached, the tears rolling down his face. He didn't even try to help, and I knew he wouldn't. It wasn't easy to get myself disentangled and on to my feet, the whole of me was soaked by that time, and no chance of being allowed to go home.

Well, it was a warm sunny day. I would soon be dry. I suppose it must have been pretty funny for the onlooker, and Dad?—well that was typical of Dad being Dad.

Between the wars we spent Christmas staying with our

Yorkshire grandparents, and two Ilkley cousins were there too. They lived in a town and we thought it must be awful for them. We found them very different from ourselves. It was many years later that I discovered how particularly nice they were.

Grandpa and Grandma had lived in a very large house in Headingley, called The Grove, and I believed I had been too young at that time to remember it, but some thirty years after the present events, I took my small daughter to a party in the Headingley area and knew instantly that I had been in the place before.

By then The Grove had been divided into two, but was still pretty grand. Entering the beautifully proportioned drawing-room, I found myself wondering why the grand piano was no longer in its place. And when we left I saw that the name of the house was still there, carved into the stone of two pillars each side of the entrance. In his letters home, Uncle Phil had teased Grandpa, referring to The Grove as "the swank house." He longed to see it, and now I wonder if he ever did.

The grandparents moved to High Leas, a house near Adel, and like most houses set in a few flat fields without farm or village round them, it looked out of place and lonely, and still does, and I can't think why Grandpa was attracted to it. Perhaps it was the beautifully mown lawn, looking like velvet between the flower borders, and perfect for playing bowls, a game he loved; but no, that would be Grandpa's own work. It must, I think, have been a desire to have a piece of land big enough to run a few cattle that was the attraction.

Years later, Dad told me that all the profit made by selling The Grove disappeared into Grandpa's many improvements to High Leas; then added rather dryly that I was exactly like my

MORE THEN THAN NOW

grandfather. When I returned to Low Hall in the 1980's and the builders were there, rescuing the fabric from dereliction, Dad's friends commented on the number of cars parked round the house, and apparently he answered,

"Oh yes, those are all Pam's friends destroying the place!"

Inside High Leas it could not have been more welcoming, the central heating intensifying wonderful smells in contrast to the cold bare polished oak at home. Downstairs thick carpets brought an almost sensual hush to the place, and Maud, the housemaid, polished large contemporary mahogany furniture till it glowed like a dark mirror.

The scent of lavender mingled with the smell of Grandpa's cigars mixed with the chrysanthemums that Brigg grew especially for Christmas in the conservatory attached to the house. In summer the heady scent of purple heliotrope permeated the rooms. Brigg was their gardener, and their Airedale terrier was called Brag; Grandma was always getting the two names mixed up, much to Brigg's annoyance.

In memory these Christmas visits have rolled into each other and I no longer remember the exact order of events, but there was always a pantomime at Leeds Grand Theatre, and I remember the excitement of going to my first.

Too young to understand the jokes, I still knew from the loud, raucous questions and audience's shouted response that I wasn't going to enjoy it and having looked forward to it so much that was a miserable disappointment! I hated the gaudy costumes, and nothing pleased until the very end when wonderful life-size fairies actually flew out over the audience throwing carnations for the children. I was almost over the balcony in my determination to catch one, desperate that the fairies mightn't see me, in seventh heaven when the last one thrown came my way and I actually managed to catch it. And then, 'oh no!'—the carnation was half dead, wrapped in crumpled silver paper and smelt horrid and I noticed the fairy had dirty feet, so could not be real.

I think I must have been five or six that Christmas, and on another day found myself with others in the large upstairs nursery of Great Aunt Beatrice's house. There was a party for the grown-ups downstairs and we children were waiting for the arrival of Father Christmas in an upstairs nursery. In he came at last in his red cloak and fluffy white beard, but when I received my present I noticed he smelled of lavender and cigar smoke, just like Grandpa, and stranger still he was wearing Grandpa's unmistakable shoes.

"Pretence fairies are one thing," I thought, "but no real Father Christmas either?!"

I had grown up at last.

Going back further, when I suppose I was about four, I remember the blissful delight of sitting on Grandpa's knee while he read to me; he felt so deliciously clean, and was always beautifully dressed in his tailored, worsted suit, stiff white collar and silk bow tie.

We grandchildren, all thought he was the best Grandpa in the world, and each of us firmly believed that he or she was his favourite. How did he do it? He had kind brown eyes with a little spark in them, tufts of white hair here and there, and a warm, deep voice.

I remember the feel of his waistcoat buttons when I leant back against his firm torso, remember too the comfortable touch of the quality wool of his suit against my bare legs. Most of all I loved the moment when we laughed together over the adventures of my favourite book, *The Animals went to Sea*.

I was the youngest of both families, and tagged along behind the others, too young to join in some of the games the older ones played, so sometimes I left them and slipped off alone to explore the house by myself.

Entering the much less used drawing-room there was an extraordinary running boy made in bronze, and hanging from his outstretched fingers hung a dried orange, pierced with hundreds of cloves, and it smelt so good I have meant to make one for myself ever since.

On the mantelpiece was a beautiful horse, the wind blowing through his feathered tail, and a shepherd astride a sheep, which I learned later that Grandpa had brought back from his business visits in Denmark.

Returning from one of his trips in the States, Grandpa's ship called in on Havana and he spent so long in a shop, choosing cigars, that the ship left without him and he had to wait three weeks before another steamer came round!

There was the gong in the hall at High Leas which fascinated me. It was dimpled and round and hung in a frame. The wooden ringer with its padded end was waiting for Maud, the housemaid, to tap it into life and tell everyone it was lunch time. The long, quivering boom noise it made wasn't very loud but carried all over the house. I longed to try it myself, but Grandma would not be pleased and I lost my nerve.

In the kitchen everyone welcomed me. Emmie, the cook, was whisking up something in a bowl on the pale deal table. Maud was polishing silver, and dear Lily, who sometimes bathed me, helping her.

From Emmie's wonderful gramophone, with its big horn and nice little dog, came the sound of Gracie Fields singing "Underneath the Arches!" and we all joined in. The long, dull leaves of Emmie's huge aspidistra rose from its glazed yellow and green pot on the same table. How could she be so fond of it? It didn't even smell very nice.

On the first Christmas I remember, when I suppose I was about three, I slept on a sofa at the bottom of my parents' bed. Dad, who did not enjoy central heating, threw open the large windows from top to bottom. It rained heavily all night, and in the morning there was a pool of water half across the floor, and I woke, appalled and deeply ashamed to discover I had wet my bed. When I confessed, Dad roared with laughter, and swore I was responsible for the lake on the floor, and for a terrifying moment I wondered if he could be right. I can still feel my resentment and hurt, a fierce compound of uncomfortable emotions evoked by his teasing.

Several aunts and great-aunts also stayed over Christmas, and all were dressed from top to toe in rustling black taffeta and grief, a narrow band of velvet round the neck, and perhaps a small brooch pinned in front in celebration of Christmas.

We found them funny and odd. We were unaware of their uncomplaining courage, making the best of the tragedy in their lives, their would-have-been husbands, lovers, brothers and sons all lying dead with thousands of others under the fields of France.

Grandma and her sister great-aunt Alice were usually found sitting together in the morning-cum-billiard room, their chairs with their backs to the light from the big bow window that Grandpa had added to the house.

Aunt Alice's brave blue eyes shone from her ivory face each side of a thin aquiline nose above an indiarubbery mouth, and I see her fine needle poised over some beautiful embroidery of strange Arts & Crafts design. She had beauty but had been born with a club foot, and she didn't like me hanging around when she and Grandma were sewing.

Dee and Buffin had stayed with her in her little house in Hastings one year and loved her, and I thought I loved her too until one day she almost spat the following words at me:

"Why have you always to be so good?" she cried. Why can't you ever be naughty?"

Shocked—I'd never thought about being naughty, family life on the farm was much too interesting and fun to want ever actually to be naughty. Her dislike of me was something new in my life and complicated things.

It wasn't Christmas at the time but when Mum and Dad were in Kenya and as there was no one at home I was farmed out round friends and relations at the weekends, and the boys had become full time boarders at Grosvenor House, like my sisters in Reading.

I was desperately homesick and missed my siblings, and of course Mummy too. Staying alone at High Leas was dull and lonely. I didn't see much of Grandpa, and Grandma sent me out in my school coat and shoes to walk the wet roads with dear Lily. We both hated it; nothing could be more depressing.

In desperation I persuaded Brigg the gardener to help me pull out the stuffed horse that lived in the little black thatched hut outside the kitchen. It was hard work, and when we eventually got him down the ramp his angry glass eyes wouldn't look at me and I didn't like him any more. He was all hard and dusty and his wheels were so small it was difficult to pull him along.

Why had he been stuffed I wondered, had he been dead Uncle Phil's and Dad's favourite pony when they were little boys? Brigg didn't know and was very huffy when we had to push him back into his little black house. I discovered I didn't like Brigg, and certainly not Aunt Alice, and realised it was the first time I had ever disliked anyone.

In a later Christmas, the boys and I were deposited at Great Aunt Mary's house somewhere in Leeds, where we spent the afternoon playing Snap. Great Aunt Mary lived with her younger sister who brought in the tea and didn't join in with our game of Snap.

Aunt Mary had a loud, authoratative voice, and announced that it was not enough to say 'Snap' we must all say 'snip snap snorum, bang galorum' when we had matched cards. This great mouthful of words put us off, it slowed us up too, so Great Aunt Mary won most of the time and we considered it the nearest thing to cheating; we couldn't wait for the car to come and collect us.

Once in the car, of course we laughed.

"Snip snap," we shouted, "bangalorum!" and thought it hilarious.

Emmie, the High Leas cook, was an excellent cake maker but lacked other culinary skills. We found the runny, half-cooked eggs at breakfast difficult, a lunch of grey boiled mutton with caper sauce just about impossible. Someone asked where the capers came from, and Dad could not resist making an agricultural joke

"From sheep of course!" and thought himself very funny. It went above the heads of our Ilkley cousins but was all too clear to me. Wet, despairing tears rolled down my face.

We children could not leave the table until we had achieved "Grandpa plates" which were polished clean with nothing left on them.

We envied our cousins who managed like the grown-ups to

whop everything down, even those awful eggs. Once they had finished breakfast, they were allowed to leave the dining-room, went upstairs and hogged the two bathrooms we children shared. By the time we got there, the smell in both rooms was most uninviting and Phil decided this was unfair and he must deal with the situation.

"No need to try and beat them to it this morning," he said. "Take your time."

When we went upstairs, the cousins were waiting in the corridor.

"We can't get in" they said. Whereupon Phil pulled both keys from his pocket and Dee and Buffin had first go followed by Phil, Gambini and myself. By the time I re-emerged the joke didn't seem to be quite so funny, and our poor cousins absolutely desperate.

Their mother, Aunty Madge, was pretty strict. She insisted I brush my teeth after breakfast as well as before and tried to make me drink a glass of water at bed time. Leeds water tasted horrible, nothing like our spring at home, so I wouldn't do it.

The cousins, Jean and Peter, visited us at Low Hall through the year, and I think Peter wished that he too could live on a farm instead of in Ilkley. He always wanted to ride on the ponies, but needed help. Bert kindly led him around, when he had time, but one day he tried shutting the gates in the stockyard and leaving Peter to it.

Peter heard us playing in the garden below and tried to see what we were doing. He leaned forward from the saddle, placing his hands on top of the wall so he could look over. The pony backed off and he was stretched between wall and reversing pony, his feet stuck in the stirrups. It must have been a terrifying moment, but Phil flew to his rescue and managed to extricate him before anything serious happened.

We liked the cousins but I hated their horrible dog called Boss who killed my rabbit. He leapt on to her run and went through the wire netting. As if that wasn't enough grief, he found Susan, my goat, tethered in the nearby field and chased her round and round, faster and faster, hanging on to her dear little tail.

I yelled for Phil who, on seeing what was happening, doubled up with laughter, but my screams were desperate, and he soon hurled himself at the dog and brought him down with a splendid rugger tackle. Susan's tail bent to one side ever after, but thankfully she still managed to wag it.

We had 'stockings' on Christmas mornings, bulging with an orange, a few sweets and little else. Then there were candles lit and crackers and turkey for lunch. The steamed Christmas pudding, all shiny and suet rich, was difficult, but must be attempted due to all the beautiful silver threepenny bits peeping out of it.

When we pulled crackers after lunch, Cousin Peter's contained a wonderful black moustache, and we all wished very much that we might have had one too, he looked so funny. We all laughed helplessly till we realised it had got stuck up his nose and he couldn't get it off. He screamed with fright and pain. What, I wondered, would happen if it had to stay there for ever! But Aunt Madge went to the rescue, and thankfully, there was little damage. I caught Phil's eye and we knew we felt the same. 'Poor old Peter! This could only happen to him!' I suppose he was about seven at the time.

After lunch we opened our parcels, just two or three each. One from our parents, one from Grandma and with luck one from a godparent. Grandpa's present was always the best, being the newly published book by Arthur Ransome, and shared by all of us.

The Christmas Tree was magical and lit with real candles, and when they burnt down all too quickly, we had the fun of blowing them out.

At three o'clock we had to stand straight opposite the wireless, while the grown-ups sat in comfortable chairs, to hear the broadcast of the King's Christmas Speech. Our poor King had an impediment and struggled a bit and the speech seemed to go on for hours. We felt the strain of being fiercely watched by our parents, all of us that is except Gambini, who, having no parents present, escaped observation and hid behind Grandpa's chair to peep out now and then pulling terrible faces! I shall never know how we managed to survive that speech!

There was a memorable Christmas lunch one year when there were exotic fruit like pineapples and tangerines and a bowl of nuts with silver nutcrackers. Everyone was fascinated by the nutcrackers, and all of us children wanted to try them out. Being the youngest of course I had to wait till last and all eyes were upon me; no one thought I would manage to handle them.

With ridiculous bravado I chose a large tough Brazil nut instead of something easy and placed it firmly in position. I knelt up on my chair with both hands gripping the silver handles and with every ounce of strength I pressed them home, again and again without success. In desperation I tried one last time. The room became quiet, all eyes watching me. Again the nut resisted, but there was a loud report from my tail end. There followed a shocked, extended silence and never had I felt more ashamed, my cheeks aflame.

That evening, Phil asked me if I had a bit of difficulty cracking nuts. His eyes were dancing with delight. 'How could he be so mean?' I thought, 'when I still feel hot with embarassment.' But when I looked again I realised he was trying to tell me not to take it so seriously but try to laugh too and stop worrying about it.

We enjoyed those inter-war Christmas but were glad when it was time to return home. Describing them leads on to the camping holidays inspired by reading the beloved Arthur Ransome books that Grandpa gave us, a new addition out every Christmas; but I must first include our one and only 'smart' holiday at Salcombe in Devon, probably in 1937.

In spite of poor Dee and Buffin developing German Measles on the drive south, it turned out to be a marvellous few weeks and all in perfect weather.

The first night when everyone was supposed to be in bed, our parents, who had hired an old dinghy with an engine from Mr Stone, decided to give it a run and make sure we would be able to manage it on our own. Needless to say we all slipped down to the sea and, hidden in some shrubs, watched them chug merrily past and expected they would soon return. But it was ages later when they came back, oars out and fighting a receding tide. They looked both hot and exhausted, and we hugged ourselves with laughter.

Next morning Dad carefully explained to us that we could have the dinghy but if it were necessary to start the engine, a certain cork must be removed first!

We bought beautifully made model sailing dinghies with adjustable sails and spent the whole holiday racing them in the harbour. No life-belts and none of us great swimmers! And what fun it was! One problem, Buffin's inevitably green yacht nearly always won. After careful inspection we discovered it was half an inch longer than the rest, so she attached two miniature life-saving tyres, one each side to slow her up, and after that winning a race was down to one's skill in adjusting the sails just right.

One day our intrepid mother decided we would sail down the coast and take a picnic, which we did, everyone except Dad who was playing golf, but Corrie our terrier came with us.

It was exciting to sail from the harbour and round a cliff to the next bay and Mummy had made a picnic so we could stay all day. When it was time to go home the tide had gone out, and our dinghy had a keel and was lying on her side, but two very friendly young men helped us to push her out to deeper water and then load us all in while they held her straight.

We waved goodbye and were just successfully turning back round the corner into Salcombe when someone noticed poor Corrie running up and down the beach, left behind. There was nothing for it but to return, and this time the young men helped us again, but perhaps, with not quite the same grace.

To return to our camping adventures, our first camp was above Bewerley, just a few miles from home and only for a couple of days. Everyone enjoyed it, even Dad, and when we came home we couldn't bear the thought of ordinary beds in the house, we wanted to pitch tents on the tennis court. Dad compromised and had Bert build a long shelter with open front below the 'drying green.' The next summer holidays we found five beds installed within it. As always, Dad had economised on the measurements and when it rained the ends of the beds got soaked, so Mummy covered them with old leather car coats that weighed like lead making it almost impossible to turn over. But that was better than having cold, wet toes!

Every night Dee elaborated on the adventures of a neighbour we believed kept chickens in her bedroom, and our parents heard our laughter and felt left out, so we discovered the shelter had been extended the following summer and two more beds fitted in. The whole family slept there, and walkers from the river path below climbed up the field to ask whether Low Hall were a residence for tuberculosis sufferers!

I would be the first to run down to the shelter, and usually found a farm cat curled up on my bed for company, but the boys soon followed, and when our ponies were in the field we three had races riding bareback in our pyjamas and I think the ponies enjoyed it as much as we did.

We still camped every summer holidays too, mostly at Bamburgh, Northumberland, and always near a golf course for Dad.

Our last camp there was in August 1939 when we found an old quarry that sheltered us from the north winds and with its close-cropped grass, was perfect for pitching our tents. Mum had borrowed an old bell tent from the coast guard which became our sitting-room/dining-room if it rained, and everything was perfect except for a mob of earwigs.

Mother wasn't much good with wriggly things so it was my job to remove all sign of them before breakfast each morning. I didn't like them either, but had no wish to hurt them so I scattered them around the walls of the quarry and naturally they all returned to the shelter of the tent each evening. They nested amongst the enamelled tin plates one used for camping in those days and, as there were hundreds, it was quite a job to get rid of them.

The next memory is so clear in my mind I will try to find words so you, the reader, can share it with me.

Picture a small child, me, sitting on top of the high walls of the old quarry. Below her, on the beach, her bother and cousin are playing cricket near the rocks where she found the special shell this morning…very rare, conker brown with blue enamelled spots down its spine.

The sea, pearly blue under the evening sky, a rippled path lit from the dying sun, stretching straight towards her. Behind and below, the grassy floor of the quarry and the rest of her family. Dad just returned from a day playing golf, talking with mother who is cooking supper on the open fire, smoke spiralling upwards with scent of sausages and bacon. A metallic clink as her sisters lay out plates and cutlery and spread out the rugs.

She smiles, picturing again the collapsed bell tent. Returning from the beach this morning, its central pole alone and naked, a mass of crumpled grey canvas on the floor. Somehow Dad and the boys got it all up again without breaking anything underneath, not even the tray of eggs nor her birthday cake.

The smell of food makes her hungry, but no one has called and the boys aren't back. She has got to wait anyway. She must see the sun dip down below the horizon, taking her childhood with it. She must be there to say goodbye.

The thought of being in double figures tomorrow brings no elation. For her, life is perfect as it is. She wishes it could stay the same for ever, but knows with frightening certainty that it can't.

She was born ten years after the end of the First World War and ten years before the outbreak of the Second. Today is the 15th of August. Tomorrow is her tenth birthday and she knows her childhood is over. Knows too, with utmost certainty, that life ahead will bring change and challenge. She knows her carefree paradise is lost forever.

Childhood in Wartime

AT THE OUTBREAK of war in 1939 some of my father's American business friends offered to have us children, and certainly my parents considered sending me, the youngest. I was secretly disappointed when they decided that the family should stick together and stay in England. Looking back, I have to think now how different my life would have been had I gone.

In the autumn of that year, evacuees, mostly from Leeds, arrived in the village by train. I walked with my mother and Uncle Mop, who had come back from Kenya and was staying with us, across the fields to wait with others outside the village hall.

We heard the train stop, but nothing else happened for a little while, and when at last they emerged from the station yard there was an uncanny silence. They walked in a crocodile, very slowly down the hill towards us. The children had their names pinned to their clothes, and each carried a little square suitcase with their gas masks hanging from a shoulder. Anxious young mothers chivvied them forward and all of them looked pale and anxious, and in need of a good meal.

Today, it is painful to remember the scene. It was so exactly like the queues slowly approaching the gas chambers seen on screen in later years.

Eventually everyone gathered inside the hall and my uncle sat at a table and wrote down all the names and addresses in a large book. Those who had volunteered to invite the evacuees into their homes hovered round, and must have been wondering what they had let themselves in for.

Many of the children who were on their own were crying and too frightened to speak, so Uncle Mop took down their details from the cards on their coats. Nearly all the girls' names were very grand, Gloria, Hermione and Miranda like the film stars of that time, and Uncle Mop smiled later and said he could not imagine anything so inappropriate for such tiny scraps of humanity.

When the record was complete, the volunteers came forward to take the evacuees back to their houses and a young mother with two little sons walked home with us. I was thrilled, especially as both were younger than myself; I couldn't wait to show them round.

Those little boys and I were absolutely convinced that the Germans were going to invade and we would starve, so the older boy and I stole potatoes from the larder and dug a secret garden in the woods. We never doubted they would grow and we pictured ourselves as heroes, carrying the crop home when the larder was bare.

All continued well until I learnt that the boys had worms. In imagination, I saw the worms squirming up from the lavatory bowl, coming to catch me. Mother reassured me that this was nonsense, but I remained unconvinced and terrified. Then there were nits in my hair and there followed weeks and weeks of twice daily washing, after which, a fine tooth comb dipped in dettol was dragged this way and that through my thick mop. It took hours, the water was cold and dripped down my neck, the black nits, dead on the white comb, the tiny eggs firmly glued to a hair. I thought it would never end. I didn't blame the boys, but life wasn't the fun I had anticipated.

We had welcomed the evacuees into our community, but it was not easy. The children who came without their mothers settled in well; it was the mothers, living in other people's houses in such strange and lonely surroundings, who were unhappy . . . the only communication with their husbands and friends, by letter. The lack of shops, particularly, fish and chip shops, the loneliness of the countryside.

Everyone had thought Leeds and Bradford would be bombed, but nothing happened; for months and months there were no raids. Almost inevitably, the mothers slipped home again, and most took their children, our little family amongst them.

After the evacuees, the Royal Engineers were billeted in Dacre, and George Sykes was the officer in charge. He and his wife Mona became our lifelong friends. The soldiers were short of washing facilities, the pub had a bath, but could hardly share it with paid guests, so Mum offered ours. She said we would take twelve soldiers every night. They must have shared the bath water, as heating was dependent on the kitchen range in those days. Soap suds surged from under the bathroom door and spilled down the landing and on down the stairs. Both floor and stairs were bare polished oak in those days.

Mother bought a thick webbing mat that fitted the room and absorbed most of the overflow, but as the weeks went by it smelt of wet khaki, sweat and carbolic soap. I had first bath after the soldiers and can smell that smell to this day, not less in my mind the blue walls streaming with drips and steam.

Mrs Don had a bath, but we discovered it was filled with coal. She used to pick up any coal that had dropped on to the lines from the trains' tender, but the coal was still considered to be Railway property. Mrs Don hid her loot in the bath, knowing it was most unlikely to be found if someone ever checked.

The phoney war, as we called it, continued through the winter, and my father was asked to visit all our neighbouring farms and report which were capable of farming cereals. He was given what looked like a large corkscrew and had to twist it into the ground. If it progressed to its full length, the field was conscripted for growing barley. Poor Dad hated the job. The farmers were his friends and he knew of the great rocks that lie just below the surface of the grass on these hills. None of the fields tested would be without rocks in some places, and ploughing them would be difficult and costly, broken plough shares expensive to replace.

He was also asked to train volunteers for the Home Guard, and many of the farmers came forward, in spite of the long hours needed in stock farming.

They were tough, hard-working, patient men, milking cows at 6 a.m., delivering the cans with horse and cart to the nearest pick-up point, then taking a dog up on the moors to check up on their sheep, before returning for evening milking. The seasonal lambing and shearing periods were especially hard, not to mention being up all night with a difficult calving. It was remarkable that just about 100% turned up to train.

Mother and I would watch from behind mullion windows, as my father tried to instill into them the basics of military drill. Country men are individuals. They can walk the hills all day without fatigue, but they found it difficult and tiring to march in time, up and down our grass tennis court. They had not been issued with rifles at that time, so used hay forks instead.

We had a small white kitten who was devoted to Dad. Inevitably it managed to appear on the lawn when these training sessions were on, and hopped and skipped immediately behind him, while he had no idea it was there. The men were helpless with laughter. I can still see Dad, exasperated and near the end of his patience, leaning down and popping the kit into his jacket pocket, all in one movement.

When invasion appeared to be inevitable, Dad divided his Home Guard into four sections and created a leader to be in charge of each area. The plan was that mother would drive her car to alert each of the four leaders, who in turn must collect their men and all get as quickly as possible back to Low Hall for further orders. No one had a telephone and few drove a car.

The alert came by telephone from Richmond at about 2 a.m., and Mother, who had clothes ready, dived into the car and drove to the first leader. The Dale was blacked out, even the car lights were reduced by cardboard insertions that seriously restricted their use. Arrived at the farm, she used her torch to find the door and banged on it loudly, but no response. She then walked round the house looking for a window and found one, so scrabbled up and through it and found herself in the larder. Soon she was at the bottom of the staircase and shouted again. At last a door creaked open and the old boy in nightgown and cap peered down at her from the landing.

Mother explained we were invaded and he must hurry and get his men to Low Hall, but he replied,

"Nay, nay Missus, I doant knaw as 'ow I joined the 'ome Guard yet."

"Oh yes you have! And be quick about it!" cried mother in her firmest voice, and departed to find the next leader.

When, eventually, everyone arrived at Low Hall, it was twelve noon next day. Just as well that the alert proved to have been a false alarum.

The only solution was to have twelve men at the ready all

in one place, and all able to rouse the rest of the troop if the real invasion came. They slept in uniform, with rifle, on twelve camp beds in our dining room. Every night they walked or bicycled to Low Hall at the end of a twelve hour day on their farms. How remarkable they were!

On one memorable night a rifle went off, and Buffin's future mother in law, Ma B., as we called her, was asleep in the room above. At breakfast she announced the news to my mother, who gallantly denied it.

"Amy dear, if you think I don't recognise the sound of a weapon being fired, when I have just arrived from Sussex, under the assault of dog fights and crashing Messerschmitts and Hurricanes, you are mistaken," said Ma B.

But my mother was undeterred; we children found the hole in the wall, but both the Home Guard men and we stuck to the story that it never happened. What was the point? A miracle that no one was hurt in that overcrowded room. There would have to have been an investigation, and it would have led to an overworked volunteer soldier being punished, and where would anyone have been found to run his farm in the meantime?

It was after the retreat from Dunkirk that Mummy invited Christopher, Ma B's son and my beloved future brother-in-law, to stay at Low Hall. Before being rescued from a Dunkirk beach, a shell had exploded immediately above him and damaged his eardrums. It was an extremely painful condition, made worse by any sudden noise; he needed somewhere quiet to convalesce. This was a second visit to Low Hall and he intended to throw his very heavy suitcase through the carriage window as the train passed Don's cottage, to save having to heave it back along the half mile walk from the station. But he miscalculated: the case rolled down a steep bank halfway through the woodland and what a job we all had finding it under all those brambles and nettles!

Our lifelong family friend John Milton was also on leave, and he and Christopher decided to meet in the Royal Oak. They did not invite Dee, on leave from the WAAF, nor Phil who was home from school, and both were a bit miffed.

There is a little mullion window immediately above the front door, where Phil, aided and abetted by Dee, constructed a complicated arrangement of pans filled with water that would empty, pulled by a string attached to the door itself. Both had forgotten about the returning Home Guard, one of whom was half drowned, and we nearly had a strike on our hands! John and Christopher had suspected some kind of reception and watched the drama, hidden in the courtyard

As soon as his eardrums healed, Christopher returned to France and almost immediately was taken prisoner and spent three long years in prison camp. Such bad luck, and we all felt very sorry for him. Buffin, unknown to the rest of the family, was so concerned, she wrote him a letter every week till the Armistice and his release in 1945.

John, on the other hand, with his Company of Green Howards, landed in France on Day One of D. Day! It is quite extraordinary that the present President of France, Monsieur Hollande, decided to award all those first day troops the Légion d'Honneur in the autumn of 2015! Some, but very few, were still alive to receive it, and sadly John, aged ninety-three, died a few weeks before the ceremony took place.

*   *   *

Shortly after the retreat from Dunkirk I was chatting with my father in his bedroom while he bandaged the wounded knee as I'd seen him do hundreds of times before. The bandage was wide and stretchy and very long. One or two of them are still in the medicine cupboard today and come in useful for a cricked ankle or sling. As we talked, my eyes were drawn to the khaki uniform on his bed.

"This time, darling," he said, "it's really serious and everyone must do their bit. I shall be leaving in a few days."

There followed a time when Mummy and I were left very much on our own. As soon as the boys were old enough to leave school they joined up, Phil in the Green Howards and Peter in the Navy. Dee was already in the WAAF and as soon as Buffin completed her Domestic Science year at Atholl Crescent in Edinburgh, she joined the Auxiliary Territorial Service.

The Green Howards had their depot in Richmond, Yorkshire, and Dad was billeted in beautiful Aske Hall nearby.

Mummy and I visited him there one weekend. We stayed in the well known Greta Bridge Hotel, and when my parents went out for the evening they left me in the charge of the head waiter. I felt fearfully grown up, sitting alone at my table in the dining room, perusing the menu, and all went well until I chose Pears in Wine for my pud. The waiter firmly vetoed the idea.

"What a mutt" I thought, "spoiling all the fun."

When Dad was moved to Northumberland, Mummy and I stayed in a miner's cottage at Newbiggin on the coast. It was one in a row of small, dark semi-detached houses, and there was a pervading smell of coke and industrial dust. It was also terribly cold, but our little room was ablaze with a mountain of coal, going half way up the chimney. The cosiness and luxury of being so warm meant that we enjoyed our stay there just as much as when we were at Greta Bridge. For breakfast

I was served a seagull's egg, which must have been a bit tired, it tasted strongly of old fish and was very rubbery and I have never been tempted to repeat the experiment.

It was the winter that Dee, now in the WAAFs, was posted to a station in the Danby area of Yorkshire, but far from the village, and on an even more exposed hillside, miles from other habitation except for a few isolated farmsteads. She was one of the first group of girls to learn the skills of Radio Location, which was the beginnings of Radar. She recalls it as a winter that never seemed to end, a time when she almost forgot what it was to feel warm. Their living quarters were a mile or two from the station, and they worked eight hour shifts and walked the distance night and day. She remembers being physically exhausted, wearing gumboots, trudging in deep snow in the dark. She slipped and fell and snow filled the boot and melted coldly, soaking woollen socks. She almost gave in, but just managed to keep on when she heard distant classical music coming from the operations building. Was the music in a dream? She was never quite sure.

Buffin was at Atholl Crescent and Phil was at Loretto, a school nearby. She was allowed to take him out at weekends and they had the luck to see quite a lot of each other. Gambini was at Trent College.

When Buffin finished the course year, she, not unnaturally, wanted to demonstrate her new-found cooking skills, and asked Mummy to buy a joint of beef. She had no idea how difficult the request was. Our weekly meat ration was very small, and Mummy was the only resident at Low Hall with a ration card. Somehow she saved up enough points to buy the necessary, but Dad, who was home on leave at the time, had no faith. He announced that Buffin could cook all the other

87

bits and pieces, but he could not risk invaluable roast beef being cooked by anyone but Mum.

Poor Mummy was caught between the two, both very determined characters. She compromised by hovering about in the kitchen while Buffin prepared the meal, and soon felt confident that all would go well.

Disaster struck when the little joint came out of the oven, and somehow turned turtle and landed on the floor. It was rescued immediately and beautifully cooked so all ended well. Dad was not informed of the accident and must have wondered why the dish became known as *boeuf à la linoleum*, amidst lots of laughter from both Mummy and Buffin.

Buffin returned to Edinburgh to join the A.T.S. and trained there. She had made friends at College and one of them had a brother called Colin. He was her first love but Colin was killed in France, almost immediately after she went back. It was some forty years later, when I was staying with her in London, that I learned about Colin. At the time I think she told no one, not even Mummy.

Mother alone

SOME TIME AFTER Dad was posted to Italy, I left Miss Walker's, having been head girl in my last year, and moved on to board at Queen Margaret's, just before I was thirteen. Both Phil and Peter were still at boarding school that year, so between school holidays, or when Dee or Buffin had a week's leave, Mummy was alone at Low Hall and had no living-in help. Everyone had been called up in the forces, become land girls, or had work in factories.

Always a good cook, Mother soon became expert at producing delicious meals from practically nothing. She also had to take Dad's place in running the farm. Don knew all the practical side of rearing Shorthorns, but it was Dad who dealt with the finances and made the decisions of what must be bought in and what sold.

Don was beloved by all the family. A Highlander and wonderful stockman, no one knew better than he how to prepare the Shorthorns for show and sale; but with all the skills in the world it can't be done without additional and specialised feeds.

Due to the war, and in particular at that time, when the superior strength of German Uboats wrought havoc on our convoys, food was short, not only for our population but also for farm animals.

Don's great faith in Mother led him to believe that she would somehow find the extras he needed, but this proved impossible and, as there were no pedigree sales, the demand for show animals vanished. Sadly but inevitably, the quality of the herd was destroyed, and when Dad returned at the end of the war he was so disheartened that he gave them up, and after Don's retirement he went in for dairy with a herd of Ayrshires.

Watching the deterioration of the herd and knowing how it would upset Dad, yet unable to do anything about it, distressed Mother as much as it did Don, but I don't remember her burdening us children with her anxieties. She much preferred to regale us with stories that made us laugh.

Mummy was a skilled and very nippy driver. She was much better at driving than Dad who treated the car like a recalcitrant horse. He was not a believer in changing gear, and would lean forwards and back from the waist up, as if he himself could will the vehicle to go up hill. Ignoring the the car's protests, progress was slow, bumpy and unpredictable. His first grandson demonstrates Grandpa in the driving seat to perfection, and reduces us all to helpless laughter, but in reality driving with Dad was always a mixed blessing.

None of our farm men could drive, so Mummy taught herself to drive the Land Rover and trailer and it was she who transported the animals to Knaresborough Market.

On one of the first occasions there were two bullocks and an old sow to sell. Don and Jack loaded the sow in the front of the trailer first and fixed a gate between her and the bullocks who were then driven up the ramp to be tied up on the other side. As always, Don accompanied mother, sitting beside her in the passenger seat.

On arrival at the market, Don off-loaded the beasts and stabled them and then came back for the sow, but she wasn't there! Don always believed that Low Hall was haunted, and he lost no time in informing Mummy of the fact yet again. Mother found herself looking into the trailer in sheer disbelief!

"We must ask if any one has seen it" she said to Don, but he wouldn't have it.

"I'll be the laughing stock of Yorkshire if we talk about it!"

"Well, let's get home, and we'll return the same way that we came and look for her en route", said Mother.

They drove slowly back, expecting to find a bloody corpse round every corner, but it was not until they neared Summerbridge that they finally came on her, grazing happily by the verge, and only a tiny piece of skin off her behind, the size of a threepenny bit. They managed to reload her and got back to Knaresborough just in time for her sale.

Near Summerbridge there is a twisty corner over a bridge, above Dowgill Hall, and on the side of every 'Rice' trailer, near the front, there is a little side door. The weight of the sow against the small door going round that corner must have burst it open and she would have shot out like a pink torpedo.

Picturing this little saga reminds me of the innate trust between man and animal that there was in those far-off days. The animals were treated with respect and patience and trusted those who cared for them. Mother and Don had no difficulty in persuading the sow to walk up the ramp and back into the trailer. It was a time when sows had straw in their styes to lie on in comfort, and, nearing confinement, they made a little nest out of it for the piglets. The animals were content and confident. The conditions were a far cry from the present day, when wet concrete is considered suitable, adequate and hygienic!

When Mr Weatherhead, our butcher in Pateley Bridge, bought one of Dad's bullocks in Knaresborough, he travelled it home and settled it in one of his fields behind the shop, or if it were winter, in a byre nearby. The bullock rested and grazed till it was needed, and at the moment of death had no inkling of its fate.

After Dad's death, I found several championship medallions in his desk, recording the success of his beloved Beef Shorthorns. However, when I started showing my Aberdeen Angus he never revealed the fact and congratulated me on my lesser successes; in fact, when we had the odd championship he was much more pleased and excited than I was myself. He was a very modest person, and now I wish I had known more of his wins and had the fun of sharing those good memories with him. He was always a better judge of stock than ever I was.

It was after Phil and Gambini joined up that home felt so different. In school holidays Mother and I rattled about in the emptiness of the house. And in another severe winter, we would pull two armchairs up close and sit side by side in front of the fire, with our feet in the stone hearth, and a bowl of porridge and cream for supper on our knees.

Before he left, Dad had arranged with Dowlings, the best chocolate shop in Harrogate, to send Mummy a box of chocolates every month, and, in spite of shortages, not to mention rationing, Dowlings never failed to send her something until Dad came back.

On the above occasion, it was a box of peppermint creams, and Mummy and I shared one cream between us, every evening. Then a tiny fieldmouse slipped from the log pile and paused in front of us to clean his elegant whiskers, and we very gently gave him a crumb of peppermint, and he picked it up in his microscopic paws, sniffed it and then ate it with much enjoyment. Every night after that he returned for his rations until the peppermints were finished, by which time it had become a much loved ritual for the three of us.

Petrol rationing became a serious issue. There was not enough for Mummy to use the car for shopping in Harrogate, so we travelled by train or bus. Railway sleepers are set just too far apart for walking comfortably and too close for running, so we learned to skip down to the station in Dacre and it was rather fun, but I feared going under the road bridge, always dripping wet and shadowed with steep, slimy stone steps up to the platform. How awful if the engine came forward and trapped us in there!

Mummy and I often found ourselves late and on one of these occasions she skipped really fast leading the way, and I saw the pretty silk cami-knickers that she always wore slipping down below her skirt. This didn't stop her, she skipped faster than ever, stepping neatly out of them as she went and then popped them into her handbag. When she opened her bag to pay for what was bought, we could see a little slip of pink silk peeping out and it made us laugh helplessly; the shopkeepers must have thought us mad.

Mummy insisted we wear tidy shoes in Harrogate, so we left home in gumboots, carrying our shoes, and threw the boots out of the window as we passed through the farm, and one of the men would pick them up for us and leave them outside the back door.

Another time we were shopping in Harrogate when there was a terrific snowfall and Mum thought it would be easier to come home by bus, the farm lane easier than sleepers lost in the snow. But when the bus dropped us off it was difficult to see where we were. Snow whirled all round us and great drifts rolled over the landscape. When we found the end of the farm lane it was blocked shoulder high. Mummy said we must crawl along the top of the wall and we did, she going first. All went well until she slipped and disappeared into a great snowy hole. I couldn't see her but heard her laughter coming up from below, and we discovered the snow was very light and fluffy and we could push though it quite easily.

Mother was a key member of the sewing group that met in the vicarage and everyone knitted comforts for the troops, once a week. The demand was such that it became a race against time, so urgent that most people took stuff home too.

All leftover wools were brought to the vicarage and knitted into squares which were sewn together to make blankets. I am not sure where they went, but certainly they were wanted.

I cannot remember why it was necessary for Mother to take her sewing-machine one day, but whatever the material it was very thick and awkward. Mummy tackled it like everything else, but the big needle went not only through her nail but also her finger, pinning it to the table. She managed to withdraw it without fainting, but only just. And the pain was as agonising as the incident was shocking.

It hurts, even today, remembering that Mother returned home that dark evening to a cold empty house, all alone.

Her annual jumble sales continued and grew too large for our dining-room, and were moved to Dacre Village Hall. There was strict clothes rationing and no one had enough points, so the sales were more popular than ever. Mother spent hours begging from friends far and wide for any clothes they could spare; then she had the difficult job of collecting them when petrol too was rationed. Thanks to her sales, Dacre Village managed to support one Barnado's child in the home in Nidd every year throughout the war and on.

Mother was still unsatisfied. She longed to do something more positive for the war effort, and hoped the house might be turned into a military hospital, but Low Hall was too small.

Nothing daunted she came up with a brainwave to advertise its facilities, and wrote out details on a card and left it in an aerodrome near York.

Her message on the card read something like this:

"Home cured ham and bacon, milk and eggs, a gun to shoot rabbits and a horse to ride. Log fires and most of all, a Warm Welcome if you wish to stay."

There were many aerodromes in the York plain and volunteer Canadian flyers manned our Lancaster Bombers. It was a time when, night after night, hundreds of Lancasters flew over Germany and bombed the industrial towns. If I remember correctly, the airmen were expected to do thirty tours before being given a ten-day respite, and the losses of both men and planes were very high. I can remember the daily reports on the news, such as "Two hundred planes successfully bombed Frankfurt last night but forty failed to return." And so on.

There was immediate response to Mother's invitation, and when I came home from school I found the house full of Canadians. They all loved her dearly and called her "Ma" and would do anything they could to help her. The house was full of laughter and fun.

I remember Gerry discovered Mother's telephone was broken, and said he would fix it, and an hour or two later, it appeared to be in order again. It was after Gerry had left that we learned the only call box in Dacre had been purloined! Mummy and I had the difficult job of parcelling it up and posting it back to Harrogate Post Office incognito.

95

It was Gerry too who intended to bring a rabbit home for supper, and I showed him round the woods. We walked side by side and Gerry carried the weapon slung between his hands, both in front of him. Suddenly it fired, and I felt the rush of air an inch from my tummy. Gerry immediately checked the safety lock and neither of us spoke, but I walked well behind him from then on. It was understood between us that Mummy should not learn of the incident.

The Canadians were great fun for me when I came home from school for the holidays from boarding school, and I half fell in love with them all. One gave me a little polished heart with a maple leaf inside the coloured plastic, that he had made from the windscreen of a Lancaster, and I kept it for years.

I was affronted when my beautiful elder sister Dee came home on leave one time, and 'my' airmen one and all abandoned me, all happily clustered round Dee! I didn't blame them, she was such a knock-out, but it was a bit disappointing.

Mummy came to know the Canadians personally. They promised they'd be back on their next leave; and some did return, but more simply disappeared. Their casualty ratio was appallingly high.

They loved their Lancasters but the planes were heavy and comparatively slow. They were desperately cold inside and there wasn't much room. The crew were bunched together except for the tail gunner who lay alone, isolated and nearly frozen, facing backwards and out of touch with the others.

They lumbered eastwards, hour after hour, weighed down with bombs. The crew knew, all too well, of possible attack by Messerschmitts. They anticipated, as they approached the target, the glare of searchlights blinding the pilot and pin-pointing their position for anti aircraft guns and knew

Mother and Father

Low Hall

Feeding ponies, July 1935

With Phil

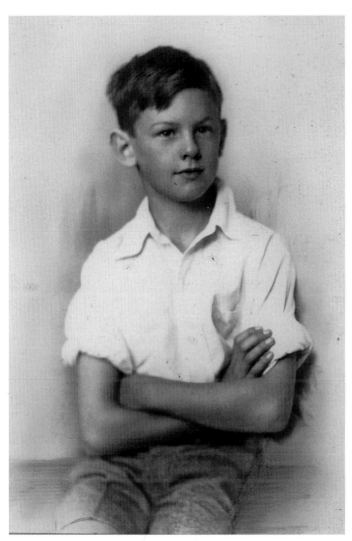

Phil

PH, Shorthorn heifer, and Don, at Pateley Show

PH and two goats

Dad's army

Phil

Shelagh

PH and Brook Holliday

Father grouse-shooting

PH, Phil,
'Gambini', Dee, Buffin
(1944)

My parents

PH

they would witness their friends shot down. What were their thoughts, I wonder, during those hours, and how long and cold the journey home, and how soon yet another foray lay ahead. I will always marvel at their courage.

When I came home the next holidays, the house was as full of Canadians as ever, and the weeks flew by. A few days before I had to return to school, I grumbled, and probably said I hated it, which wasn't strictly true, but home was so much more fun.

"We'll come and see you!" said the Canadians, "We'll come and beat up the place." And they did.

I was playing Lacrosse on the cricket grounds that afternoon, when the great plane surged down on us, so low, everyone fell flat on their faces. It thundered and lumbered over us, then, as I watched, it headed straight for the Castle. It seemed to hesitate, almost stop, before with a roar of accelerating power it lurched desperately skyward and by inches missed crashing into the high scaffolding that supported the fire-damaged dome.

I shrink from the memory of that incident, even today. What should have been a marvellous moment, waving a 'thank you' to my Canadians for their visit, grips me with the horror of what so nearly happened. Especially that the cause of a so nearly terrible accident stemmed from the Canadians' kindness to cheer me up. I see the plane again and again, too low, too close to the dome, and realise it was only the pilot's skill, his split second reaction, that saved his crew, the plane, the Castle and everyone inside it, from tragedy.

It was much later that I learned that an oversight in the design of the Lancasters' cabin, meant the pilot had very restricted vision of anything close up, which for some reason only adds more shock to the memory.

When I was home for the next holidays, Cecil, pronounced 'Ceecil', was there. My sister Dee had done some work in Mr Archie MacIndoe's Sussex Hospital, and through this connection, he decided that Low Hall and Mother would be the best place for Cecil to recuperate between the many operations he must undergo.

Mr MacIndoe was one of the first—if not the first—surgeon to develop the skills of skin grafting, and Cecil, who was a young American, had been the tail gunner in an American plane that broke up as it crashed, killing the rest of the crew. Cecil was very nearly burned alive. His burns were so terrible one had to wonder if death might not have been preferable, but that was before one got to know him. What was left of his face was bright red and puckered. He had no eye-brows nor eye-lashes, and no nose. His hands were like little claws. Mr MacIndoe was rebuilding his face with skin grafts taken from other parts of his body, but dried blood on his sheets revealed that his legs were as burnt as his arms and hands. The only parts of Cecil that were not impaired were his courage and good cheer.

He insisted he go down to the village pub on the day he arrived, and people in Dacre were appalled by the sight of him; they and we had never seen anything so very shocking before.

I suspect Cecil walked straight into the bar and ordered drinks all round. If he did, that was the only beer that he ever paid for in the Royal Oak. From then on, through all the months he spent with us between the operations, he was given free drinks. He became a much loved Dacre mascot, and it was extraordinary that everyone's shock at his appearance disappeared, we soon grew to love him for what and who he was. Mummy would wait up for his return each night, and when he arrived with his new nose, that stuck out from his face much too large and very white, she was not in bed before midnight. Cecil rolled in at the back door grinning from ear to ear.

"It was a job, Ma", he said, "It took all night to achieve, but look…the tip of my nose has turned pink!" And it had.

The relation between Cecil and the Canadians was civil rather than friendly. They were all volunteers, but Cecil was conscripted, and the USA had taken an unconscionable time to decide they would join in and fight. Cecil's concern was that Mother might tell the Canadians he had never actually been in battle, which was something of which he was deeply ashamed. The plane had crashed on a practice flight. Mother never said a word of course.

After what must have been another two years the War was over and Cecil was well enough to go back to the States. He wrote mother one letter saying that he was to be married. It was marvellous news, and we thought she must be a very special girl and prayed that they would be happy.

For several years Mother received letters and Christmas cards from Canadian families, thanking her for welcoming their sons into her home during the war, and the boys themselves kept in touch too.

Castle Howard

DURING THE FIRST WORLD WAR three German destroyers entered Scarborough harbour and shelled the largest building in view, which happened to be a girls' boarding school called Queen Margaret's. There was little damage but, when WW2 broke out in 1939, it was decided the school must be evacuated and it moved, almost immediately, to Castle Howard.

There were five children in the Howard family in 1939, three sons and two girls. The boys were of an age to join the Green Howards. Their sisters, Christian and Kate, moved out of the Castle and lived in the Gate House, and Kate became a schoolgirl in her own home while I was there.

Sadly two of the brothers, Mark and Christopher, were killed in action, so it was George Howard who eventually came home to live in the Castle after the war.

I arrived in the summer term of 1942 when I was twelve, and was the only new girl in my house. The girls were friendly enough but, having been in school since the previous autumn, they had formed established friendships and I felt like some kind of extra. There was an American girl in my dormitory, however, who was different from the rest, and she infuriated Matron due to being so untidy.

Matron appeared in our room one night and harangued her for a solid five minutes before running out of steam, but the girl, whose name I have forgotten, kept her cool and said quietly.

"Have you forgotten, The Lord saith *Let not the sun go down upon thy wrath?*"

And Matron retreated, like a ruffled broody hen, and I laughed and decided I liked the American immensely; I think we would have been friends had she not left at the end of the term.

Castle Howard, the place itself, went straight to my heart. I was thrilled by its grandeur and wonderful architecture, the beautiful gardens and lakes. I revelled in being free to explore the grounds and very soon found myself walking the sun-hot sward that leads to the Temple of the Four Winds.

A delicious scent of thyme filled the air and I picked some, just one of all the other wild flowers underfoot: clover, selfheal, cinquefoil, milkwort, veronica, eyebright, crosswort, and many others. On the unmown banks each side of the walk, I found wild scabious, campion, geranium and sorrel and, looking down to the lake, I saw it was massed with cream water lilies spreading out and across like a mantel of old lace.

A dozen or more figured statues accompanied the walk, most with a bullet hole in its side, supposedly shot by a stray German pilot, but the site, so far inland, made me wonder if the temptation had not been too much for one of our own.

Back in school I could find no vase for the flowers, so borrowed a dinner plate and short-stalked them into the drop of water it afforded. Several girls said how pretty they looked, but not one wanted to know their names, and I thought how odd this was compared to Miss Walker's, where knowledge of wild flowers was a priority.

I was desperately homesick and, although this was unspoken, Mother must have known, as she raised no objection to Susan accompanying us in the car, when she drove me back after half-term.

Susan was my goat and I had spent half-a-crown on her purchase. She was my War Effort; if our old house cow died, goat's milk would 'save the day.' Her previous owner, Mr Myers, was in charge of the road verges in and around Heyshaw. He scythed the grass and his little family of goats clustered round him and grazed while he worked. What grass was left over he made into hay and carried it home to feed them in winter. When Susan was old enough to be weaned, Mr Myers delivered her to Low Hall on his bicycle, with Susan skipping along beside him on the end of a string.

Susan lived on the now unused tennis court and had a hen-house below the laundry at night time. She came for walks like a dog and generally enjoyed life. Dad sent me invoices for use of his land, and I charged him for mowing, and 'chain harrowing' the lawn and keeping it in good condition, but after lengthy and cheerful correspondence from both parties, we agreed a truce and no pennies changed hands.

When Susan first arrived we thought she might get a chill on rainy days, so Mummy made her a splendid raincoat, with a yellow and white checkered lining created from an old bath mat.

At Castle Howard there was a groundsman who lived in a cottage near the cricket pitch. I told him of Susan and he said it would be no trouble for him to look after her, so she rode quite happily in the back of Mum's car and we dropped her off at his place, before arrival at the castle. Having her there, and being able to visit her, was a great comfort for me during the second half of my first term.

A year later, the headmistress summoned me to her room and I feared the worst, but such a relief when she said there was a telegram for me.

"Twin daughters arrived, all well, love Susan."

"Your sister, I presume" said Miss Brown.

My first dormitory was on the ground floor overlooking

the stable yard. Ten iron beds each with a locker, small chest of drawers and narrow hanging cupboard filled the space, but in contrast, the short inner wall had ornate shelves supporting layer after layer of beautiful leather bound books that rose to a wonderful cornice of acanthus leaves. Another surprise was a short flight of steps in one corner that led to a bathroom. This was a great bonus for us but I could not imagine the original purpose of the room, the head housekeeper's or butler's perhaps, but why all those books?

One night I was woken by the sound of a Lancaster bomber flying low. Everyone could recognise the sound of a Lancaster, the engine had a particular rhythm, but this one was in trouble. The beat was slowed then stopped, started up again and seemed to struggle on, then stopped again. I held my breath and prayed for the crew in the brief, ensuing night silence, then heard the ghastly thud of its crash close by.

The other girls slept on undisturbed, and the quiet breathing room belied the horror of what had happened, I knew with a terrible certainty that any crew still on board must have died instantly and when morning came I spoke of it to no one. What had happened was beyond mere conversation, and I too shocked to face the questioning.

It may well have been Half Term in the following winter that Mummy wrote to say she hadn't enough petrol to come for me and take me home, so she had booked into a little pub in Sheriff Hutton and we would spend the time there. It was a very raw, wet weekend with icy winds, and the only place provided for us was a small, cold bedroom with double bed, no fires or warmth anywhere. We were thankful for the double bed, it had a feather mattress and heavy blankets and eiderdoon, so by sharing we warmed up eventually.

Each morning we braved the elements and looked round the ruin of Sheriff Hutton Castle in freezing desperate weather, cold rain, icy winds, threatening low cloud, then thankful to be back in the little pub, we shot upstairs and read books, fully clothed in the double bed. I don't remember where we found food!

That term everyone had chilblains both on fingers and toes, and we brought back from home large tins of Germaline which was supposed to suppress the nasty stinging hurt that chilblains exert, and to this day I cannot bear the smell of the stuff.

Most girls in my form had plenty of tuck which was kept in a locked cupboard in the Common Room and opened on Saturday by a prefect, for rationed distribution. Mother did not know about being allowed tuck, the other girls seemed to have got their parents lined up somehow, but that wasn't something of which Miss Walker or our family would have approved, so she never knew. I remember crowding round like the others pretending I was expecting my name to be called, I didn't want anyone to know that I hadn't any chocolate etc.

In my second term I was voted form captain, and without a thought I initiated some of the Miss Walker standards, and the girls came 'on board.' as though it were a game, certainly a novelty and rather fun.

For a week we were less boisterous and more considerate and courteous, but all too soon my ideas were considered a great bore and within a couple of weeks the initial enthusiasm wore thin, then completely fell apart. No one was unpleasant about my ideals, they all seemed to continue to like me, but any authority I may have held was lost for ever.

Instead of swimming, we had gym lessons in the autumn

term and I had no idea what to do but hoped I'd get away without anyone knowing, if I watched carefully. Seeing the girls rapidly scaling the ropes, it looked easy enough, and it was, but how to get down again? I had no idea! So I just let myself slide and the rope took all the skin off my palms. The pain was harsh, like a burn, but rather than look a fool I pretended it hadn't happened and tried to smile my way through all the other activities.

Unlike today, with its exquisite planting of specie rhododendrons and azalea, under magnolias, designed by Jim Russell, Ray Wood was a wild place of scrubby trees with brambles and nettles underfoot.

It was out of bounds, but it reminded me of the much more beautiful woods at home, and I spent hours exploring there and climbing trees; I liked to sit on a branch and read a book, and no one in authority appeared to notice where I was nor where I went. It felt good to get away from the crush of so many girls. I was used to tagging along with Phil and Gambini which I considered much more fun.

At the top of the wood I found an enormous hexagonal trough, its walls topped in beautifully dressed stone. It was something important but I could only wonder at its purpose. It was some forty years later, when I had the luck to be invited to Castle Howard on the day we would see the fountains come into play again, that solved the puzzle.

After a splendid lunch in a marquee, we guests stood outside and waited for the moment. Suddenly both lakes erupted into dramatic cascades of water, so beautiful to see, it caught one's breath. And I understood at last the purpose of the stone trough at the top of Ray Wood.

I am not sure for how many long years the eighteenth-century lead pipes had lain lost and broken underground, but it must have been a huge and delicate operation to restore both them and the rams that took water from both lakes up to the trough from where it was released through pipes back to the fountains. A most successful invention of perpetual motion.

In summer I discovered we must swim in the fountain centred on the south lawns of the Castle. It is beautiful and very large with a bronze statue of Atlas holding up the world. At his feet are dolphins, spouting water into the decorative, shallow pond below, and we had to swim like a swarm of gold fish round and round. One girl in our form dived in and knocked herself out on the bottom!

Once the weather was warm enough, swimming took precedence over Gym and, whatever the temperature of ensuing weeks, we had to bathe, and stay in the water for at least ten minutes. On wet days we shivered forth, wrapped in our cloaks under umbrellas.

Our bedrooms, where we changed, were at least ten minutes away from the fountain, and as soon as we were allowed we dashed back and tried to get dry and re-dressed in time for the following lesson. We were in trouble if late, and it was no fun sitting through a forty minute class in a large cold room with wet hair soaking one's collar and dripping down one's neck.

It often resulted in 'flu' and a spell in the san. There was one term when I caught mumps, measles and chickenpox simultaneously and then developed bronchitis. The overworked nursing sister was incensed that I forgot to bring hankies with me and said she had not time to get them herself. I couldn't bring myself to use the sheet; I lay with a high temperature, in semi-darkness, nose stuffed, and forced to breathe through my mouth for two or three days, and have never forgotten such misery. Mummy however was granted extra petrol to take me home, and as soon as I knew I made an almost instant recovery. To her disbelief she found me outside the san. and running headlong to meet her.

In wartime school food was pretty disgusting and there was not much of it. Cracked enamel dishes, like one's dogs' bowls at home, arrived, filled with watery dollops of grey meat that I can only think was horse. It had the strangest, sweetish flavour and I found it difficult to get it down. One never saw an egg— sometimes breakfast was of reconstituted, dried egg powder, served on top of corn flakes. Friday lunch permeated the entire castle with a strong smell of stale fish before it emerged into the dining room in great yellow chunks with thick, shiny black skin. The only food I could eat happily was at elevenses. We queued in an underground passage and were served with a piece of stale bread spread with beef dripping. We never had anything remotely like roast beef so I have no idea from where the dripping came, but compared with all else it was delicious, and I couldn't get enough of it.

In the winter terms, we got chilblains both on fingers and toes, and they itched painfully, week on week. The only treatment in those days was Germaline, but it didn't help much. I came back in the autumn, stacked with tins of the stuff.

When I discovered Spanish Chestnut trees produced little nuts, a small version of the sweet chestnuts one buys at Christmas, I collected them and peeled off the prickly casements, made a little fire of twigs and, using the lid of my Germaline tin, I fried the nuts in a tiny cut of butter saved from teatime. The miniscule feast was well worth all the effort, and I told my friends how to do it, but no one joined me in foraging for nuts, and no one was interested in collecting dry sticks for fires.

There was a period when I found the long line of temporary 'loos' in a lower floor passage unacceptable. Our headmistress had a room on the first floor of my 'house', and at the other side of the landing was her very comfortable bathroom. Knowing her routine. I was able to avail myself of the latter, throughout all the years that I was at school, and was never found out.

I was lucky to have had Miss Walker's preparation behind me. Work was no problem, and I still enjoyed lessons in spite of moderate instruction. Apart from English and Maths, our lessons were uninspiring. People of call-up age were fighting the war, so our teachers were middle-aged and tired. Against that, both Gym and Lacrosse were new to me and excellently taught by Miss Donaldson, until she too joined up. I loved both, and still believe Lacrosse to be the most graceful and exciting team game that there is, certainly the fastest on foot.

There were, too, plenty of things to enjoy at Castle Howard. Unconsciously I absorbed the harmony and quality of Vanbrugh's grand designs, both inside and out, and fell in love with all things eighteenth-century.

When I became a house prefect, I qualified for the use of a first floor room, where, in winter, there was always a fire, and I remember many evenings curled up on an old couch, deep in Galsworthy. Sometimes I just sat, taking in the beauty of the room, its ornate Italianate marble fireplace, or just looking round at the family portraits, elaborate cornice and beautiful proportions of the room, though I would not at that time have been able to put it all into words. Outside on the south lawns there are still the enormous, carved stone urns, big enough to carry craggy viburnums grown into small trees, and then, centred beyond, the lovely fountain with Atlas holding up the world. It was a privilege to be there, and the glory of English Baroque seeped into my soul and has remained an interest all my life.

In my form in senior school, Lady Mary Howard looked down at my desk from her portrait—a happy, smiling girl in harebell blue dress, a diaphanous sash swirling round her. I enjoyed her presence and firmly believed the smile was for me, wishing me well.

I loved the richly ornate chapel, singing in the school choir, and sometimes reading the lesson. But in one unforgettable term the whole of the Castle became infested with rats. I never saw one, and the problem was quickly treated with poison, but it made the rats thirsty. The chapel organ operated on a water pump, and the poor suffering rats were drawn to the scent and died in their hundreds under the marble floor. The stench was intolerable. We all trooped in with hankies held to noses, twice a day and for an hour on Sundays. And why, I wonder, when the Castle had a wonderful first-floor assembly hall which would have served just as well for a few weeks. But not one of the staff considered the possibility and, in spite of one girl actually fainting, we carried on in the chapel.

In April 1945 peace was declared, and I found myself hasting up the narrow, stone spiral staircase that leads to the Castle roof. All the girls with me were hilarious with joy, but something held me back. I could not feel as they did when Dad was in Italy, my sisters in the Forces miles away, Gambini out at sea, and our brother at OCTU (Officer Cadet Training Unit) in India. And Mum was all alone at home. It was too soon to celebrate. I was glad to leave them to it and slip back to bed.

I think it was about this time that Mummy received a parcel from Italy inside which she found silk stockings, not seen in England for nearly five years, and a beautiful crêpe silk dress for me. It wasn't until Dad came home a year or more later that he told us where he had found these lovely presents.

Much to his disappointment Dad had not been allowed to serve in 'the front line'. He was put in charge of a mule train bringing up supplies as the Army advanced further and further north through Italy. The European war was nearly over when he found himself just outside Florence, and slipped across one of its bridges to find presents for the family. It was on his return to the camp that he became aware of notices everywhere with orders to remain in camp. It had been discovered that Florence was still alive with both German and Italian snipers left behind to inflict what damage they could!

Gravitating to senior school brought one or two benefits, but I was always homesick for the first fortnight of term. Once those two weeks were under my belt, there were only eight or nine more to get through before the next holidays, and the calculation made life more bearable. It is true too that as I moved up I enjoyed school more, and made friends with two girls in my class, both called Sheila. We became a kind of trio. We all loved playing Lacrosse and were in the team, and they were good at tennis too, but I wasn't. I made it to the cricket team and thought I was quite a nifty bowler.

Another interest was piano lessons. I was taught by a gentle, elderly teacher who filled me with confidence, and progress was good and rather exciting, but unfortunately I was promoted to be taught by the head music teacher, who was too much for me. She made me terribly nervous and sadly I gave it up. I remember listening to a cello sonata, curled up under a grand piano for some reason, and knew clearly I should have learned to play cello rather than piano. It felt much more 'me'.

I continued with ballet and was chosen to produce the Hall House ballet in competition with School House, and mine depicted the story of Ondine, a sea nymph.

Although the European War was over, clothes rationing continued to be a problem, so Mother bleached our 'black-out' curtains many times until at last they faded to cream, then she re-dyed the material back to a soft blue green. She cut it out and designed simple tunics that were very effective and exactly what we needed, in spite of their throat-catching stench of bleach.

School House 'went first' and produced a more ambitious ballet, and I was hugely impressed and sure that they would win, but to my delight we beat them. I had chosen Elgar's 'Chanson du Matin' for the music and it was ideal for dancing and also in tune with the story—hearing it played today never fails to fill me with delight.

I was made a House Prefect when I was fifteen, and was pretty sure I would be Head of House one day. We were working for School Certificate, that led on to 'Highers' which, after another two years, should qualify us to enter university. I thought I would read English, or possibly History, once I got there.

After the Armistice in 1945 the summer half-term fell in June, and Mother wrote that Dee was coming home on leave, and Gambini too was being let out from the Navy. My heart sang, it would be like the old days, at least four of our family together.

And it was just like that the first day. Friends came in for drinks, and Gambini looked great in his uniform, smoking his pipe filled with a handsome allowance of Navy tobacco. I was impressed, remembering how sick he was when we children smoked in our 'river cave.' Then I noticed he had left the large tin of tobacco open on a low table, and when Susan, my goat, walked in to join us she swiped the lot. Gambini only pretended great indignation, he laughed good naturedly, and I suspect he was thankful. The pipe was all 'show,' he had probably left the tin out for Susan on purpose.

The next day was a perfect summer's day and Gambini and I played 'cricket' on the lawn, and Dee did a bit of fielding. Mother lay in the sun on her chaise longue, in front of the French windows, the wireless nearby. No one moved anywhere in those days, without taking a wireless with them.

I swiped a high, fast ball which shot back across the lawn, struck the wireless and smashed it into smithereens; and at that moment my world turned upside down. I found myself alone in an unimagined world of darkness and terror. I could see someone who was me, still in the sunshine, with mother, her arm round me, saying,

"Don't make such a fuss darling, it's only a wireless and we have another."

But that was a dream. The real me was in this place of darkness and terrible pain. Alone within its shadows, I saw it overwhelm everything in life that I loved most, and watched it lay waste my world.

Dee walked up the drive with Gambini when it was time for him to catch his bus. I don't think I even said goodbye to him, I remained trapped by a fear I hadn't known possible.

Dee and I shared a bedroom, and next morning we woke, hearing Mummy running up stairs, and she came in holding a telegram which had come from India.

"Phil's ill," she said, "he's in hospital. He's got some unpronounceable disease I have never heard of."

Dee flew downstairs to find a dictionary and when she returned she read out the symptoms of poliomyelitis, and I still hear the sound of the points of Mummy's shoes drumming on the linoleum, as she knelt at the side of Dee's bed, her head in her hands.

A day or two later, another telegram came and we read that Phil was holding his own.

A third telegram arrived and Phil was a little better, and on that note, I went back to school.

Later in the week the headmistress sent for me and told me my sister was coming to see me, and I could go out for tea with her.

Dee arrived with a friend, who turned out to be a distant cousin from South Africa. He had volunteered as a fighter pilot and some missile had punctured his fuel tank. He tried desperately to nurse the plane back to the Allies' side of the battle, and failed by only a few yards. After months in a German prison camp he had been released as far as London a few days previously, and came up to Yorkshire to meet us before returning to the Cape.

We were having tea in the village café when they told me Phil had died. The telegrams from India had arrived in the wrong order. Phil died on the Sunday of my half-term.

A few tears flowed, but nothing dramatic; the terrible pain, horror and grief had happened last Sunday. Now a hateful numbness, heavy as lead, arrived inside me.

Conversation was hopeless. Dee and Geoff drove me back to school, and someone told me to sleep in the 'san.' The numbness made me feel desperately tired and I went out like a light. I woke, and felt deeply ashamed to find I could not cry. In fact I felt nothing at all except for the painful heaviness inside that blotted out all joy.

No one spoke to me, except to say I was to sleep back in school the next night.

A nice girl, Pat George, had wept buckets when her brother was killed. For days one heard her running along corridors, roaring loudly, her mouth open and the tears splashing down her face. I couldn't do it, I couldn't even grieve. I went back into school and behaved as though it hadn't happened, as though everything was the same.

Inwardly nothing was the same. My friends, even the two Sheilas, were out of reach. Overnight, I seemed to have grown years older, leaving everyone else behind, and to the new me their behaviour was silly and childish, and that included the staff. None of them seemed to know anything about the real world.

Neither the headmistress nor my housemistress approached me, in fact no spoke to me about Phil and no one sympathised. I wonder now, if they thought at all, it was that I didn't care.

If I could have gone home and been with my Mother for a few days, I think my grief would have come out naturally, and I would not have felt so alone, even if Dee had had to go back to her station in Cornwall, there would have been Bert, Don and Jack on the farm to share and understand my grief.

My escape was in work, and I worked hard. I was taking School Certificate at the end of term, and I wanted to do well. Working was a relief; the concentration took over, and I could lose myself in it.

I took the exams, and knew with certainty I had done well. For most of them I remained at my desk, and Mary Howard, from her portrait, smiled down at me, the only person that understood the ache in my heart.

It must have been a good summer in 1945 because when our School Certificate exams finished we were left to our own devices for a couple of weeks before the term ended, and I remember lying out on the warm, short turf of the south lawns in front of the castle, reading in hot sunshine, alone, but more at peace, worked out, satisfied.

I determined that nothing would stop me from doing well in the next two years. I would go to University, and I couldn't wait. Somehow our family would learn to live without our beloved Phil.

Dee and Buffin would soon be coming home, and perhaps, Gambini too, and surely Dad wasn't needed in Italy now that the European war was over. Our house would be filled once again with the sound of voices. We could still be a family again. But nothing turned out as I hoped and it wasn't long before I came to accept that nothing could be the same, ever again.

I have little recollection of the summer holidays that followed Phil's death. Mother and I were pretty close; we had shared so much during the past few years and lived harmoniously together, but I don't remember being able to talk about Phil.

The memory and loss seeped deep into our lives, a wound that would not heal. I worked on the farm a bit, and enjoyed helping where I could. Bert and both Don and Jack welcomed me home and their friendly company was comforting and reassuring in my changed world.

The Canadians had gone home but Mother had lots of letters, not just from them but also from their families, thanking her for taking care of them.

Gambini was demobbed and opted to be returned direct to

his beloved Kenya and be with his family again. There was a new sister, whom he had never met, little Lynette, the only girl after four boys.

Dee was demobbed from the WAAF and was working for Mr MacIndoe (Cecil's surgeon) in Sussex, organising concerts and other entertainments for his patients.

Peter Browning came home at last from Afghanistan. He and Dee had been apart for four long years with very little communication. Few letters actually got through from Afghanistan, and on his one attempt to telephone the line went dead before Dee reached it. I had answered the phone and Dee said it was all my fault, and perhaps it was. I was thrilled to hear his voice and wanted to know when he was coming home. Dee accused me of not shouting loud enough. Be that as it may, we all knew the wicked old biddy in charge of our local exchange always listened in to our conversations, and this call from the other end of the world was probably too much for her, she could easily have pressed a wrong button in her excitement.

When at last Peter and Dee met they discovered that they had grown up into different people, and the romance failed. It was a very tough time for both, but it was Dee who ended it, Peter was truly heartbroken.

To go back to Phil, Peter Browning's coaching had got him up to the Loretto standard, but in his first year he developed scarlet fever from a wound to his eye when playing rugger. It needed stitching and went septic. He was seriously ill and missed almost a whole term. It meant he had to work very hard to keep up for all the time he was there, but this perhaps made him popular and much liked by staff and boys, especially as he succeeded against the odds.

Dr. Greenlees, the headmaster, loved Phil and later, at the Loretto Memorial Service, he spoke of his grit and determination to succeed. I don't remember anyone who didn't love Phil.

Dee married Geoff, the distant cousin from South Africa who had come to Queen Margaret's with her to tell me Phil had died. She spent her gratuity on a trip to Kenya and travelled on to the Cape, where Geoff met her, and they became engaged and a truly wonderful marriage followed.

Buffin married Peter Browning's elder brother Christopher. She must have met him when he stayed at Low Hall recovering from injuries received during the retreat from Dunkirk. Buffin was the first in our generation to get married.

My sisters never returned home properly. They married from home and dropped in now and then, but soon both went to live in different parts of South Africa. Christopher taught Classics and Rugby in Saint Andrew's boarding school in Grahamstown, and Dee went to live on an enormous fruit farm near Elgin, in the Cape, where Geoff was a manager.

I could not have had nicer brothers-in-law. Geoff became a constant and beloved ally for me and had I come to know Christopher better, he would have been the same. But when I needed them and my sisters most, all four of them were far away.

I still dreamed my dreams, still believed we would find a way through all the sadness one day, and life would be happier again.

We had all loved Phil. Dee remembers seeing him off to India from London. They had lunch together and Phil insisted he would pay the bill. The meal was bad and the service worse, but the sweet, a kind of ice cream called Bombe Surprise,

117

cheered the end. Then Dee, elder sister, noticed Phil had not left the waiter a tip and reminded him.

Phil replied.

"Well that's his Bombe Surprise." And Dee still laughs remembering it.

Buffin and Phil shared the fun of Pony Club camps when they were young and then saw much of each other when she was at Atholl Crescent in Edinburgh and he at Loretto.

I remember Phil best when he and I shared our childhood after the girls had started school, and I still treasure the letter he wrote to me in the brief period he was in India, telling me how much he was enjoying life and what a very special Indian person he had been given to look after him, who wore a 'teddy bear' overcoat every morning, and I would like him too.

In our way we all relied on Phil, he was the key that bound the family together. It was Mother who wrote up his short life of eighteen years. She gave us each a copy, and it is a slender, small, white book, embossed with his initials in silver. It is a book that makes one both laugh and weep.

For the first time I was glad to go back to school for the Autumn term of 1945. It would be easier than home, where at every turn there were reminders of Phil and Mother's courageous determination to hide her grief and carry on.

I found myself part of a group, all moving forward into two years of study that would prepare us for University, and for the first time I integrated totally, without reservations.

Mother wrote that at last Dad was coming home from Italy. It seemed extraordinary that, with luck, he would be home in time for half-term. Then I heard he had arrived and was to come to see me. How lovely, I thought.

Immediately he came, he said we were to have a meeting with the headmistress, and I found myself following him up the staircase to her room. The meeting was brief, there were no smiles, and we remained standing.

Dad asked if I would get into Cambridge.

"No," replied the headmistress. "Many young people are being demobbed from the Forces and War Work, so naturally they will be given precedence to finish their studies that have been interrupted by the war. There will be few if any spare places left. She would have to be truly brilliant to have a chance."

Then Dad said, "Well none of those red brick places are any good, are they?"

"No, I agree, they are not," replied the headmistress.

Her words struck all purpose out of my life. And something in me died and I felt it go.

Neither Dad nor Miss Brown had looked for a moment in my direction. I heard them say they thought I was too young to leave immediately. It would be better if I continued till the end of the school year. They gave me no opportunity to speak and Dad returned home immediately, without a backward glance.

I wandered back to my class stunned, all hope of my planned future wiped out of me.

It is difficult today to realise how completely subject the position of the child could be, versus the adult, in 1945. It did not cross my mind that I could appeal.

For me it was the knowledge they thought I wasn't good enough to go to University that was so painful. What more could I have done to show them I was more than capable?

I tried to believe they must know better than me, but knew they were wrong, wrong, wrong.

I believe Buffin would have rebelled but she and I were very different in character. She had not shared my idyllic childhood, which engaged loyalty and unquestioned love for our parents. She was courageous and single-mindedly determined to make a different kind of life for herself.

Sadly I didn't rebel. School became a nightmare, my group totally involved in study, while I skipped lessons and was caught reading a novel in the warmth of a linen cupboard, when I should have been doing something with the juniors, and in consequence had my prefect's badge removed. I determined I didn't care.

I felt alone and terribly lonely. I became deeply ashamed, feeling I had let myself down. It hurt to leave school when the time came, knowing that, if they remembered, no one would think anything of me, and I lost all self-confidence for years.

Tanrego

IT WAS DIFFICULT to know Dad's thoughts when he returned from Italy. He had left Low Hall a vibrant place, alive with five growing children, and came back to find it empty and bereft, but he allowed nothing of his distress to emerge in visible form.

I believe, however, that he felt everything that he had striven to achieve was now lost. Due to the death of his only son, there was no successor for the thriving business he and Grandpa had built up, and no one left to inherit Low Hall. I think he was in a state of terrible despair.

Phil's death brought back the death of his heroic elder brother who had won a posthumous V.C. in the First World War. He had named Phil after him in honour of his memory, and now he too was dead, and all hope gone.

He was brought up as a Victorian and could never have considered that one of his daughters might be capable of helping in the business; he believed marriage was our role.

Grief had changed his beloved wife, and he felt he no longer knew where her thoughts lay. They had been apart so long and each had learnt to cope with grief in their own way; and now it was too late to change.

Dad upset Mother terribly by suggesting Phil's death would have been more bearable had he died in battle, and this is the only time I remember our mother, always so loyal to her husband, but now so hurt and embittered by the remark, breaking down and repeating it to me.

I wonder now if Mother had disapproved of the way that Dad had pulled every string he knew to avoid Phil being a

Bevin Boy. When it was time for his call-up, Britain was desperately short of coal and needed more men to work the mines. The Minister of Works, Mr Bevin, solved the problem by taking a proportion of the new call-ups and sending them down the mines instead of into the Forces. It was a lottery that Dad was not prepared to risk. Somehow he managed to ensure that Phil joined the Green Howards ahead of schedule.

Mining was dangerous and an honourable alternative to the Army. Had Mother, I wonder, thought of this at the time? If she did, I pray that it never entered Dad's head, before or after Phil died. But still, I wonder.

*   *   *

With Low Hall wracked with hidden tensions and misery, I was as desperately sorry for Mum and Dad, as I was for myself. The solution was to take a holiday. The three of us would go to Ireland, where Mother had some distant relation, and I welcomed the idea. I had never heard of Aunt Eva, who lived near Sligo, but that wasn't surprising after five years of war and all the family scattered.

We spent the first night at the Hibernian Hotel in Dublin, and for dinner we were placed on a table next to a riotous French rugby team, celebrating victory. They were served steaks so large that they flopped over the edge of the plates, and the boys ate ravenously, swopping chunks of meat on their forks and laughing hilariously. At home, each of those steaks was double the equivalent of a week's meat ration. We had forgotten that such abundance existed, and ordered smaller portions for ourselves. Scrumptious they were too, but even Dad could not manage to get it all down. How I wished we had had our dogs with us.

We stayed a further couple of nights in a very grand place,

turned into a hotel. It had two lakes in the vast grounds. Its name escapes me, but I remember how lonely and sad it made me feel. There was little enjoyment in wandering about by myself; my parents at least had each other to share its magnificence.

The journey to Sligo took longer than expected. The roads were small and twisty and not well marked. We stopped and asked a roadman if he knew of Tanrego, and he did. We were on the right road and it wasn't far. Mother asked how long it would be before we arrived—she was fussing we would be late for lunch—and he replied,

"Ye'll be there in no time, just a mile or two."

In fact we were a good hour away and didn't get there till after 2 o'clock, by which time Mother was pretty desperate, but needn't have worried. The beautiful old house stood there, basking in hot sunshine, the welcoming front door wide open, and not a soul in sight.

We wandered round and discovered a little beach close by, with sailing dinghy drawn up on the sands, and a glorious view across Sligo Bay. There were old stables, with a few horses within, and everything there neat and tidy. The untidy stockyard and hay barn beyond had a cluster of hens sunning themselves in the yard.

It must have been twenty minutes later that Uncle Gordon quietly emerged from the house to meet us. He explained that Eva had forgotten the sherry and had gone down to the village to buy some, and she would be back any minute and, as he spoke, her car shot up the drive and, just like a busy little hen herself, she ushered us into the house, bottle and all.

Lunch appeared towards three o'clock and halfway through Willy slouched in, helped himself from the sideboard and without introduction settled himself in the empty chair next to mine. He was middle aged and tough, not someone one would wish to take on, and his intrusive presence wove itself into the fabric of Tanrego's many secrets.

Conversation flowed, mostly between Aunt Eva and Willy, and was all about horses and prospects for point-to-pointing, and Dad was fascinated.

Uncle Gordon ignored Willy, he never addressed him nor looked his way. Dad tried to bring Gordon into the conversation by asking him about the farm, but Uncle Gordon was not forthcoming, not even about that.

He was a dear man, so shy he hardly spoke a word, but Aunt Eva never stopped and relied on Willy to back her up.

Mother asked Eva why the roadman who had directed us, told us that we were only a mile or two from Tanrego, when the distance was so much further.

"Oh," she said, "he wouldn't want to disappoint you."

In spite of our odd reception, and the unusual hours, we fell in love with Tanrego and both Uncle Gordon and non-stop-gossipy Aunt Eva. In their way they made us very welcome and we learned there were four daughters, and the two elder ones were famous point-to-point riders. We discovered just how delicious was hot soda bread made for breakfast in the Aga each morning. How it soaked in the wonderful home-made butter. It was a warm and friendly place.

Aunt Eva bred the horses and thought of little else; they, with Willy, were her world. Kathleen, the eldest daughter, told me later that her mother had stripped the eiderdowns from their beds one cold winter's night to put on the horses she thought were sure to freeze in the stables.

Uncle Gordon's interest was centred in sailing. He had built the beautiful dinghy we saw on the beach and at every opportunity he slipped away, to be seen far out, a small white sail, seeming almost to fly, back and forth, in the blue waters of the bay.

The weather broke and there were several rainy days, and Dad noticed there was mown grass lying wet in the bottoms of Tanrego meadows

Then we were back to fine weather again, a morning of light breezes and sunshine. At breakfast Dad turned to Gordon and said.

"Well, at last, a lovely day to get that hay turned and dried, it'll save the crop!"

And Gordon replied,

"And a perfect day for a sail."

Dad shook his head in perplexity, not at all sure which held precedence for Uncle Gordon, but suspected the latter.

*   *   *

It dawned on me that my parents were to leave after a few of days, but I was to stay for a month, and Aunt Eva would instruct me in riding.

There must have been a financial agreement, but Aunt Eva had no intention of keeping her side of it. I think she was frightened I might fall off and become a real nuisance; she must have starved poor Patsy Fagan, a half backed filly, into docility. When I took Patsy Fagan out, always on my own, she could hardly put one foot in front of the other. She hadn't enough energy to trot, and after the first session or two it became extremely boring.

Uncle Gordon came to my rescue. He took me out sailing and taught me a bit about it too. We became friends and the days and weeks flew by. Home again I talked of nothing but the joys of sailing with Uncle Gordon, and was surprised to discover that Dad did not appear to be interested.

Porlock and Sheilah

TONY COLLINS's riding-school in Porlock was, I believe, the first of all the hundreds of similar places dotted round the country today. He based the training on the Military Equitation Courses at Weedon, and created a school for students in Porlock, and another for short weeks of more specialised teaching in Porlockford, where he lived.

When Dad came to hear about the place, he sent me there as a student and we drove down to Somerset together, spending a night with Aunt Irene en route. Having to face the long return journey next day, the parents dropped me off at the school early and I thought myself alone until I bumped into Sheilah, who was also exploring our accommodation in the pretty thatched house provided.

Sheilah was a year or two older than my seventeen years and had been born in India. She didn't talk much about herself. It was bit by bit I learned that the father she adored had died young, and her widowed mother, who was working for Intelligence, arranged for her to go to boarding school in South Africa. Perhaps there was little alternative but Sheilah hated the school, hated the family with whom she lived, and was desperately unhappy. The trauma being so extreme, those were wasted years; she learnt almost nothing other than a remarkable courage upon which she would rely for the rest of her life. As soon as she was old enough to leave, she returned to India.

She then volunteered to drive a Land Rover stacked with 'comforts' for the troops fighting in the Malayan jungle, and on one occasion her 'team' had found themselves behind enemy lines. They lay low for two days and nights, hardly daring to breathe, before the Japs lost the ground they had gained and retreated.

She had always been very small for her age and looked young for her years. She had a mass of soft wavy hair, which she hated and tied back in two thick bunches when I met her. She was graceful, elegant and brave, very determined and a great companion.

"Let's go down to the sea," she said.

It was a stilly, warm afternoon and nothing much moved as we walked through the village of whitewashed, thatched cottages and little shops, and turned right towards the beach. There was not a breath of wind, and I thought how lovely and inviting the place was in contrast to the bracing, chilly coasts of North Yorkshire.

Far out we saw a figure returning from a swim; he came slowly towards us, barefoot and gingerly on the cobble beach, and it turned out to be Dick Hern, recently demobbed after fighting in the Italian Campaign.

He and Sheilah talked naturally, but I felt embarrassingly shy, he was so marvellously handsome, a towel slung round wet shoulders.

Most of the girls on the course fell in love with Dick, who was great fun and an excellent and amusing instructor in the school, but he was having an affair with a pretty local girl at the time, so out of reach.

The other students had turned up by the time we got back from the beach, and the house was buzzing with the noisy activity of arrival. Hunting boots, heavy with their wooden 'trees', crashed on wooden floors, followed by laughter and shouted instructions as the owners sorted themselves out.

The course itself turned out to be quite tough and physically demanding. We had to muck out and feed a horse before breakfast under the sharp eyes of Mr Ffitch.

"Fitchy" as we called him, was a stickler for high standards but the dearest man, bow-legged, leather skinned and lined, always humorous, he never missed a trick. We used to laugh and say he had 'turkey legs and bees' knees' but if in distress, he was always there for you.

The stables were some distance from the village. I remember running for my life down a high walled path under the branches of an old mulberry tree that in July splashed squelshy ripe berries on all and sundry and tasted like the sweetest and richest raspberries. Beyond, there was a bakery where one was assaulted by the smell of newly baked bread; food was still rationed and we were always slightly hungry. In no time I had arranged with the baker to leave a bag of buns on a window sill for us to pick up as we passed.

It was almost impossible to buy oats to feed the horses at that time, and Tony Collins bought broken biscuits from a factory nearby that made them. I remember some had pink and mauve icing and I couldn't resist eating a few myself.

The horses we rode were of every description, from the odd thoroughbred to carthorses. Dairymaid was one of the latter. She was a great romping, dapple grey, with short thick neck and mouth hard as iron. She was willing and vigorous but would not, perhaps could not, canter. We were taught in a big covered school, and rode different animals every day and always hoped for anything but Dairymaid.

A retired Colonel was the other instructor and he had a short temper.

"Prepare to canter!" he barked, while we learned to 'sit

down at the trot' round and round the school, and everyone would adjust their weight to help their mount lead off with the correct foreleg into a slow collected canter. All that is except Dairymaid, who romped round in great leaps and bounds but still at the trot.

The Colonel shouted us to a halt, told Dairymaid's rider to dismount, and climbed aboard himself to demonstrate. He and Dairymaid set off round the school, and faster and faster they went, but still trotting. The Colonel lost his temper and whacked her with his whip to no avail. He whacked so hard he broke the whip and borrowed another which he also broke. Poor Dairymaid was in a muck sweat, and so was he, but still only trotting. At last, purple in the face, the Colonel dismounted and walked briskly and furiously from the covered school; as soon as he had gone we all collapsed with laughter and no doubt the poor man must have known.

Dick was the only person who could get Dairymaid to canter, except perhaps Sheilah who was by far the best rider in our group. She had a way with animals; both horses and dogs always wanted to please her. One could see how much she was enjoying the course, quietly following instructions and carrying them out to perfection. She was happy with everything at Porlock except for the overcrowded and noisy accommodation.

"Let's find somewhere else," she said.

"But where?" I asked.

"Well, that little place might do."

We were walking down the main street in the village at the time, and where it curved to the right a small thatched butcher's shop stepped out on the left, and thus faced back up the street.

Portly Mr Lear beamed from behind his counter, expecting

a sale. The shop was stacked high with all kinds of meat and game and it was beautifully kept. There was an inviting smell of fresh lard and much highly polished brass and copper hanging from the walls.

He was somewhat put out when Sheilah asked if he had a room to let, and said he must ask the wife. We could hear them discussing the proposition for some minutes before dear Mrs Lear bustled in, looked us up and down and then asked us to follow her.

Through a low door at the rear of the shop there was a little twisty staircase with shallow oak steps that led to a surprisingly large, airy room under the thatch, and between two windows looking on to the street and only a few inches above the level of the floor there was a low double bed.

"I think its large enough," said Sheilah. "May we try?"

Mrs Lear laughed as Sheilah pulled out the bolster from under the white, starched coverlet and placed it down the middle. We lay each side of it and found there was ample room. From that day on till the end of the course we stayed with the Lears.

There is something of the fairytale to sleep on a feather mattress, so soft and light, as was Mrs Lear's unexpected appearance at six o'clock every morning with a cup of tea and home made lardy biscuit in the saucer.

A girl on the course approached me and said she hadn't thought I was a lesbian, and I hadn't the faintest idea what she was talking about, but knew, instinctively, this was sticky ground.

"Oh really?" I said and dashed off.

By the end of the course, Sheilah knew everyone in Porlock, and they knew and liked Sheilah.

I went home but she managed to get employment as a secretary and shared a little cottage with Pat Pope who was studying and instructing Dressage at Porlockford.

I popped back to see them and stayed in the cottage at some point, and managed to fit in a wonderful day's hunting with the Devon and Somerset Stag Hounds.

South Africa

In the late 1940's Philip Denis Kilpin was born, and he was our parents' first grandson. Buffin had already produced two little daughters in Grahamstown, South Africa, but neither of my parents seem to have thought it necessary to travel out to see them, and it is only now, writing about it, that I realise how hurtful this must have been for Buffin and Christopher.

Mother and I sailed on a Union Castle steamer to the Cape, but to everyone's surprise, and slight concern, Grandpa was determined to see his first great grandson too. Grandma had died in a car accident some time before and her last wish was for Great Aunt Alice, her sister, to move from Hastings and live at High Leas to take care of him. The wish was dutifully carried out, much to the chagrin of both parties; they had never liked each other but believed they must keep a promise which made their lives much more unhappy.

Phil's arrival was the means of temporary escape for Grandpa, and Dad decided he must accompany him and it would be better for Grandpa to travel in a 'flying boat' which took only four days. It was not a good plan. The craft had to take off and land in the still atmospheres of early morning and late evening, the days were too long and the nights too short, neither had slept well and they arrived looking tired and worn out.

The Cape summer didn't suit Grandpa, he found it too hot and sensibly removed the stiff collars he always wore and, much to Dee's shame, firmly refused to put them back on, whatever the formality of an occasion. Denied their smart collars and with only a stud at the neck, his beautifully hand-made shirts looked like any other, and Grandpa somehow appeared to be wearing a working man's garb. But Grandpa was a charming and very disarming person, and if anyone thought his outfit unsuitable, they never said so; only Dee complained.

In those days a voyage to the Cape took some eleven days, and for me it was a first and became a glorious adventure. There were games on board and a swimming pool. We danced to a little orchestra in the evenings or strolled on deck under a great dome of starred sky, warmer than a Yorkshire midsummer.

Soon there was the delicious aroma of hot sun on salt tarred rope and almost white wood deck, too hot for bare feet. One woke to the soothing swish of soft brooms sweeping the decks in the cool early mornings. Everyone played deck quoits and swam in the large swimming-pool. Crossing the equator was made into a cheerful ceremonial occasion, and I shall never forget seeing the load of fresh bananas taken on board at Teneriffe. We hadn't seen a banana for five years! In the restaurant I delighted in foods unknown and only the custard apple disappointed when a large grub shot out of it just as I took a bite.

Life on board was wonderful and like nothing I had experienced before. I was happier than I'd been for years in such paradise and even Mummy looked more like her old self.

On arrival, we found the little family in a high state of drama. Dee, very hyped up, her bosom all swollen and tight and obviously tender, Geoff standing by, and their baby squirming on Dee's lap, roaring with hunger and frustration.

Geoff suggested that his little son must be blowing rather than sucking, and after a brief moment of shocked silence, we were all laughing helplessly, even poor Dee.

Mother knew exactly what to do and in a short while, a satisfied infant was tucked up in his cot and peace reigned. Mother was smiling, in her element; she had come alive again at last.

Geoff and Dee's house was tiny. Mummy and I slept on the stoep outside, just a roof over our beds, it was like sleeping in the shelter when we were children and, of course, quite the best place to be in a South African summer.

When things settled down, it was decided that Mummy and I should drive the 800 miles to visit Buffin, before the arrival of Dad and Grandpa, and we borrowed Geoff's old Plymouth car for the trip. It had a broad springy bench across the front and very little room to put anything behind. I was too young to drive so Mummy had to do the entire journey, not that it worried her, and we arrived at Beacon Island in great form. The hotel was full but we found a simple B&B in the village and left our suitcases and everything else in its one room.

It was already evening so we flew down to the sea, with a perfect, natural beach that stretched for miles and not another soul on it. As the sun went down we danced and sang from sheer joy. There was white sand as far as one could see and the bluest of waves rippled in the hot bright sunlight.

After years of war and deprivation in the cold of Yorkshire we felt we were in heaven until darkness came down on us so quickly we could hardly see where we were, with only the lights of the big hotel way above us for guidance.

Walking to the beach, we had stepped through high banks of reeds which Geoff had warned might hold snakes. The only thing that really terrified my mother was snakes. We crept back, hopefully in the right direction, and I went first, but fear is infectious and we hardly drew breath till we found ourselves on the path back to the village.

It was a relief to be in the street again, but house curtains were drawn and this was our first experience of the solid, black velvet of a South African night. The village had no street light, and nothing moved. We walked up and down trying to find our room. Eventually we were drawn to the dim blue glow outside what we discovered was the policeman's small house, and he was happy to pilot us back. Without our telling him, he knew exactly the room where we were staying. It had no lock and its door opened on to the one street. How lovely and how lucky we were to have been in the Cape when it was as safe and happy as any other civilised country at that time.

Hardly, if any, of our route was tarred, and one had to discover the right speed to drive on the dirt roads whose surface became ridged and patterned by the elements. We drove many miles next to a railway line, and Mother kept saying she heard a train approaching, but it never came. At last she stopped just to check and discovered the rhythmic 'chuffing' was caused by a completely flat tyre on a rear wheel.

We had never thought to ask Geoff where he kept the puncture kit, nor where we'd find the spare wheel, and now we could not find either. We hadn't passed a car for hours but before we had time to feel anxious, one rolled up with four young men in it. They were not only delightful but also super efficient. They unzipped the spare wheel from the back of the wide front seat and found the tools tucked in there too. We were back on the road and waving our thanks in a matter of five minutes.

It was lovely to see Buffin and Christopher again and the babies were darling. They had a dear young nannie who sang to them in a sweet, low voice that told of 'Xosa fairy tales and customs and I can still sing the first line of one of them.

They lived in the town and had an enormous avocado tree in the garden, laden with fruit, but the climate was degrees hotter than in the Cape. It was difficult to sleep, I found the nights stifling and remember the awful wailing of thousands of street cats quarrelling and mating on the roofs of neighbouring houses.

One evening, listening to the news on the wireless, we heard of riots in Durban. We were hundreds of miles from Durban, but I saw that Buffin was frightened by the news, and wondered about it.

My ground-floor bedroom was away from the rest of the family and, English fashion I threw open the big window hoping for cooler air. I lay, trying to read late into the night and became aware of footsteps on the path outside walking stealthily nearer and nearer. My heart stopped, as indeed the steps did, just outside my window. Then there was a terrific crash as someone leapt through into my room. This and the news of riots were all too much, I shot down my bed under its single sheet and waited to be murdered.

Nothing happened and I couldn't stay there for ever. When I managed to come up and open my eyes, dear George, Buffin's large Dalmation, was gazing at me. He'd returned from an illicit jaunt and found himself locked out.

I got sunstoke in Grahamstown and spent a few days in bed with high temperature, and all the skin on my back came off. I had been invited to the nearest beach on a dull and clouded day; I hadn't realised you could be sunburnt when no sun was visible, and the experience wasn't much fun. I loved seeing Buffin again and playing with those babies, but I was glad when it was time to go back to the Cape.

Dee and Geoff had masses of friends, amongst them Dickie and Brian, both of whom had volunteered in the war like Geoff. They were going on a fishing trip to the Wilderness where Dickie's mother had a house, and they invited me to join them. I couldn't believe my luck.

The boys were fishing for blue point shark at night and caught several. I had one on for a while but failed to land it. We fished for hours from the darkened beach but managed to spend some time in the one and only hotel to dance. In early mornings we climbed rocks at low tide, and 'slurped' for oysters using old penknives. They were delicious, eaten immediately, squashed between thick white bread and butter. We put the surplus catch in a little bucket to keep them fresh and took them home to Birdseed, Dickie's mother, who cooked them, and made a delicious sauce, and we ate them for supper. I don't remember when we slept, but suppose we must have done at some point.

They taught me how to fish for Leervis and I managed to catch one. It is a fish that lives on others, so one needs live bait to attract it. The Leervis descales its victim before swallowing it, so the fisherman has to let it run free on the line, giving it time to do this before lifting the rod to check it.

First we had to catch the live bait, and Brian had a weighted net for the purpose, and Dickie had brought a very large torch.

We went out at night to the lagoon which was bridged by the railway. Dickie walked carefully overhead, on the sleepers, which were screwed directly on to a couple of huge RSJs and nothing in between...if you missed your step you fell straight into the water below, and of course it was dark.

Dickie shone his torch down on to the lagoon, and Brian waded quietly below. The torchlight attracted a shoal of harders, fish rather like herrings, and Brian swung his net high overhead so that it flew out into a circle before touching the water and sinking down. It was beautiful to watch such artistry and very exciting for me who had seen nothing like it before. He successfully netted hundreds of harders and Dickie was so delighted he forgot he was balanced on the sleepers and fell off. He plunged feet first into the lagoon below, a drop of some thirty feet, and only about four foot of water. The torch kept its light so we could see where he was.

He was terribly shocked, and we had to haul him out and wrap him in any spare jackets we had to warm him up, but by some miracle he was still alive and not seriously injured.

We three got on so well we couldn't bear for the holiday to end. We drove back to Elgin and didn't stop. We drove over Sir Lowrey's Pass and on down to Gordon's Bay and had a midnight swim. The boys had no idea what a rotten swimmer I was and I never thought to tell them.

In the dark, great rollers were coming in, and the idea was to climb aboard and surf back to the beach. But I found myself inside the roller. It was lit with pale green phosphorus within and it tumble rolled me on and on for what felt like hours, until it finally deposited me on the beech.

How lucky the tide was coming in and not going out. I didn't try again, and soon the boys had had enough and dropped me off at Dee and Geoff's in the early hours. It was too sad to say goodbye. I just slipped inside, knowing I'd had the best holiday of my life.

Mr Downer

THE HUNTING SEASON was over, and I was glad. It was Spring, everything in the valley was 'greening up,' and I decided I must learn about gardening.

The Greenwoods lived a few miles south of Low Hall in a hideous Victorian pile, built in the middle of their estate, which had an equally horrid name of Swarcliffe, but a beautiful garden round the house, and large walled garden too. I knew it well, because I had lunched there occasionally.

The Greenwoods had three sons, and the youngest, Johnny, and I were friends. Col. and Mrs Greenwood, always kept a fox or two for the York & Ainsty Hunt. I will never forget the sight of Mrs Greenwood on her perfectly turned out Skewbald cob. She, feather light and neat on top of his eager, gleaming, muscular form, made an unforgettable picture and I admired and loved her. Col. Greenwood, in contrast was a long angular figure on his much larger hunter and because he rarely spoke a word to anyone, he was known as Chatty.

I was invited to lunch now and then, and think Mrs Greenwood still hoped that at least Johnny would take to riding, and between her and Dad plans were arranged that I should ride over, and Johnny meet me halfway. We met alright, but it was at the edge of the garden woods, some couple of hundred yards from the house, and Johnny would be standing there, beside his pony, lazily smoking a cigarette. He'd open the gate for me and then climb aboard, and we'd ride back to the stables, where Smart, their groom took our mounts and stabled them.

At lunch none of the boys nor Chatty spoke a word, and

for me it was astonishing when at home I could hardly get a word in edgeways. So I tried manfully to break the silence. Mrs Greenwood backed me up, and when Chatty's old, black Labrador picked up his bowl and carried it round the table like Oliver Twist, begging for remnants left on our plates, I managed to get a few words out of Chatty. I've often wondered since what the boys thought of my performance.

I assumed they were terrified of their father, but years later someone told me that it was Mrs Greenwood who was the tigress, and now I shall never know which.

All three boys had gone when I arrived at Swarcliffe to learn about gardening, Chatty had died, and Mrs Greenwood was often away, visiting Billy, the eldest son, who was farming in Australia. It was obvious, however, that she had left strict instructions regarding the formalities that must be observed between myself and her staff.

Dad had given me the filly I had ridden at Tanrego, and part of the arrangement entailed that I must ride to Swarcliffe. Now full of oats and life, she was an unpredictable ride, and bucked me off regularly. The sandwiches I prepared for my lunch were squashed flat and often decimated to a pile of crumbs by the time I arrived. We had to negotiate a knacker's yard en route, and sometimes I thought I'd never get her past it.

Smart, the groom, was always waiting for me, and touched his cap and said "Good morning, Miss 'irsch," to which I replied, calling him Smart.

Smart stabled the mare and rubbed her down, and I carried my knapsack to the Hall and knocked on the front door. Smith, the butler, opened it said "Good morning Miss 'irsch", and relieved me of my knapsack, adding that he expected me to return for lunch at 12 noon.

That first day, the weather was perfect, and I ran down to the walled gardens filled with delightful expectations, but arriving at the potting sheds there wasn't a soul to be seen. I had been told that Mr Downer would be expecting me. There was nothing for it but to sit and wait, and a wave of disappointment swept through me.

After a mystifying wait of half an hour, three men emerged from some hiding place and shyly introduced themselves. I didn't know it then, but they had nearly gone on strike at the thought of a girl upsetting their routine.

Mr Downer, the head man, was the quietest, gentlest person I had ever met. He set me on to thinning the unwanted tiny grapes spread across and under the sloping glass of a greenhouse. One had to do it with small pointed scissors, without touching the larger grapes in the bunch. Bright sun splashed itself through the glass. It was a hot, awkward job, working just above eye level, and I had also to scrape the branch stems to kill off the chance of red spider. I didn't stop working till I had finished this unpleasant job, some three days later.

It was then that they accepted me and we made close friends. Gordon, just married, was always laughing and making jokes, but a good, fast worker. Poor Tommy was very slow and always making mistakes, and Mr Downer in a quiet way kept us in order, and taught everyone what gardening was all about.

I must have made a good job of those grapes. They were Muscat and unbelievably sweet and delicious when it came to harvesting them, and I think sold in Harrogate. Mrs Greenwood was in Australia again at the time, and I remarked to Mr Downer how sad it was that she wasn't at home to enjoy them.

"Well," he replied, "we'll keep back a couple of the best bunches and give them to her as a Christmas present." He then showed me how to put a piece of sulphur in two wine bottles half-filled with water, and then place them on a shelf upstairs in the potting shed. The shelf had a lip, so the bottles lay on their sides with the top sloping back to the bottom. We cut the grapes with about a foot of stalk; it was vital that the grapes must hang free and touch nothing. The plan worked beautifully, May Greenwood was as delighted with the present as she was surprised.

It was 'down tools' at elevenses time and both Smart from the stables and Smith from the house came down to share mugs of tea brewed by Mr Downer and have a good gossip. They were all mad about racing and betting and talked of little else. I, the student gardener, was 'Pam' in the gardens, and quite unconsciously became 'Pam' to Smith and Smart, and was delighted. But when I collected my knapsack from the Hall and mounted Patsy Fagan, saddled and bridled by Smart and ready to return home in the evening, I was back to "Miss H."

I made one memorable mistake when Mrs Greenwood was to arrive back from a summer visit to Australia. Without asking Mr Downer, I picked every single sweet pea that there was, and arranged great vases full of them, round her drawing room to welcome her home.

Mr Downer nearly fainted, the sweet peas had already been sold to Miss Campbell's, the smart florist in Parliament St. in Harrogate.

"I'll lose my job!" he gasped. "Miss Campbell will be just as angry as Mrs Greenwood, and what can I say?"

"Don't worry, Mr Downer," I replied with more confidence

than I felt, "it's all my fault, so if anyone is sacked it will certainly be me."

Mrs Greenwood didn't speak to any of us about the mistake, and I was allowed to continue in the gardens as before, but neither did she thank me for her homecoming surprise.

The other amusing picture that comes to mind refers to my so-called lunches. I would return to the Hall at noon and Smith would let me in to the huge, oak-panelled hall centred by a large, highly polished Victorian table, gleaming with a finely cut glass jug of water, and an equally ornate tumbler, typical of the 1920s. Beside them there was faultless silver cutlery with salt and pepper, and piled in the centre of a magnificent china plate were the remnants of my sandwich. It felt rather lonely, nibbling like a mouse all by myself in a depth of heavy silence and no visible life. Smith never reappeared until on my way home he waited at the door to return the battered knapsack.

Mr Downer and I became thick as thieves. He and his wife were childless and wanted a cat, and I found them two black and white kittens that cheered them up no end. He taught me well, and his gentle, kindly tuition lit my life-long passion for gardening,

Needless to add I would love to have stayed on for the full year, but all too soon it was cubbing time, followed by hunting, and there was no escape from either.

Drifting

TOWARDS THE END of summer the horses came in from fields to be stabled and prepared for the hunting season, and secretly my heart would drop. 'Back to the old grind' were my thoughts, as I struggled to groom Patsy Fagan and clean her 'tack'.

My father and most of the people I knew were full of anticipation, and although I enjoyed hunting too as recreation, I resented it being a full-time occupation that blocked out time for more interesting pursuits. I could not commit to this overwhelming dedication, but could not bring myself to say so, knowing how disappointed and upset my father would be. My 'aloneness' grew with the years. I felt a fraud pretending I was something I wasn't, and in a later time I learned that keeping such a secret preoccupies one's thoughts to the point of debarring one from making friendships. It is always there, but never revealed, never spoken.

Gardening and being taught how to sow seeds and take cuttings, caring for growing things, had lifted my spirits. I would have much rather have continued to work at Swarcliffe than hunt.

Miss Walker was short staffed, and invited me to help out, teaching the seven year olds. I rode my autocycle to Ripon two or three days a week, and discovered I loved teaching. As with gardening, one was helping something to grow. Miss Walker asked me to stay on, but Dad, without putting it into words, made it clear that I had a hunter, and that must come first. It would not have crossed his mind that I had never asked for a hunter.

He was generous in so many things and loved to hear about my skiing trips, and I loved skiing much more than hunting.

145

It was simpler: one took one's skis out before the holiday and then they went into a cupboard and waited for the next year; whereas having hunters was a continuing responsibility.

It was my job to check the horses every day during the summer, and I woke one night, remembering I had forgotten to do so. They were in The Dip, a field at the other side of fifty acres of woodland, but there was a full moon, I didn't need a torch. Entering the woods I heard the most ghastly sounds and thought an old tramp must be gasping his last. It was frightening but one couldn't just leave him to it. I crept cautiously towards the dreadful, drawn-out, guttural groans, and wet coughs, to discover the noise came from two little mating hedgehogs!

The night was of a velvet softness, warm and friendly, the little hedgehogs made me laugh. I wouldn't have known about their habits except for the hunters, just as I would never have seen the wild daffodils in Farndale, nor massed, clumps of primroses under dancing catkins, remembered in Ryedale. Even they were not enough, however, to still my unending hunger to be educated and qualified to do a proper job. Denying the hunger left me with low self-esteem and devoid of self-confidence.

Skiing and other rather wonderful holidays lifted me out of myself temporarily and I remember the joy of them and the fun I shared with non-hunting friends.

Due to post-war austerity one could take only £25 abroad, so we skiers had to accommodate ourselves round these difficulties. A friend and I mustered nine people each to form a group of twenty which achieved remarkable price cuts. Thankfully one was able to pay for travel while still in England, and we booked group tickets for third class journeys.

We travelled through the long nights, sitting on slatted wooden benches in continental trains, packed together like sardines, with our luggage, too bulky for the narrow overhead shelves, round our boots and on our knees. Being agile, I climbed up on to the racks above our heads and stretched out flat. They were comfier than they looked and I slept well, but no one else thought of doing the same.

We booked the whole of a tiny hotel in Leck, Austria, and lived on bread, hard-boiled eggs and garlick sausage, and carried the food in haversacks on our backs. There was masses of deep snow and few tracks. Using skins on our skis, we climbed the mountains before skiing down them, and we loved every moment, it was like being in heaven. We danced in the village hall every night, still wearing our boots and ski clothes, as continued clothes rationing at home left little choice. We were always hungry, but extraordinarily happy together and our group continued through succeeding winters.

Another year we stayed in Kitzbuhel itself, where there were basic ski-lifts, just a wooden anchor on which one leaned back with one's great flat wooden skis pointing uphill, in front. Most of us fell off on our first attempts and had to go back to the end of the queue to start again, but the lifts were wonderful to get you up to the top, once you got used to them.

Rickhardt was our instructor, a delightful old man who gave us his all. It snowed heavily that year, and on our last day, when we had saved up to ride in the more expensive cabin lift, and were all aboard, a loud voice on the tannoy advised not to ascend.

Somehow we persuaded Rickhardt to ignore the warning, and up we went, passing the final descent of the cabin coming down. It was too late to change our minds.

147

Getting out at the top, great, soft, snowflakes swept past us horizontally and so thick we couldn't see our feet. It was extraordinary not to know if one was moving forward or back or just standing still.

Rickhart gathered us round him and brought out the bottle of gentian, giving each a little glassful of the harsh sweet liqueur. It went down well and also went to our heads. By the time he got the bottle back in his haversack everyone had disappeared.

Flying swiftly down, down, and half blinded by the snow was one of the most exciting experiences I remember. We all made it and poor old Rikhardt was much relieved to find us still in one piece and together at the bottom, but I fear he had a lot of explaining to do and nearly lost his job, for having allowed us to go up in the lift.

Another year our party landed up to find our accommodation was a loft over a herd of cows. At least it was warm, and the animals were bedded down on clean, sweet-smelling, dried bracken. It was almost romantic, but we were some distance from the slopes and our breakfasts and had to trudge half a mile across the mountain to find both, and that was not so good.

Ireland and Sheilah

A YEAR OR TWO after Porlock, Sheilah came with us to Ireland, where we stayed once again with my mother's distant cousins, who lived in Galway.

Horses were still Aunt Eva's domain and Uncle Gordon, who had built himself a beautiful little sailing dinghy, escaped from the farm, horses and family whenever possible. We'd see him, out in the bay, beyond recall.

He was quietly fascinated by Sheilah and I was so glad he approved my friend, but could not help feeling a little envious, finding myself outside their natural field of communication. Now I can see it was Sheilah's Irish genes instinctively bonding with his, two like spirits, both vulnerable, both alone in their worlds.

There was much talk of the coming Dublin show, and Sheilah was dying to go. Without quite knowing how, she and I were invited to stay longer, so we could have a day in Dublin en route for home; perhaps it was Uncle Gordon who got us the tickets.

A heavenly summer day dawned after a week of rain when my parents left and we said our goodbyes and watched the car disappear down the drive. We had a few more days in lovely Tanrego, our flight tickets home, our tickets for the show. How good life was.

On the day we were to leave, Aunt Eva was in a fuss. She insisted we must have boiled eggs for breakfast to sustain us on the journey, but there were no eggs in the larder. Everyone was in the hay-yard, searching, Uncle Gordon already in the car, waiting. At last someone found a nest in the barn and we swallowed hot eggs almost whole and flew out to him.

When we saw the train's smoke swiftly weaving across the flattish countryside, he put his foot on the accelerator, but to no avail—we tore on to the station just as the train pulled out. It was the only train that day, we thought we would miss the show! But no, Uncle Gordon had a word with the stationmaster and arranged that the Sligo-Dublin Express would wait for us at the next station. Back in the car, we sped across country again, and yes, there was the train, puffing smoke impatiently by the platform, and breathlessly we climbed aboard.

Sheilah adored the show, and wanted to stay another day. Why not cash in our air tickets and take the ferry tomorrow evening? In no time she had organised the switch. I have no memory of where we spent the night, but we enjoyed having time to see more of the wonderful show and, thoroughly worn out, we caught the ferry on the following evening.

It was packed, not a seat left under cover, and the weather turned cold. There was nothing for it but to stay out on deck in summer clothes without protection from the elements. A kindly young man offered to share his rug and we gratefully accepted, and huddled down on deck for the night.

It was in the warm train to Petersfield next day that we discovered we were alive with fleas. What was worse, the cash had gone, and we had no money to pay a taxi to take us to Sheilah's grandparents. She telephoned and explained the situation, and a grumpy Mr Tweedie agreed to come for us.

We were not allowed to enter the house. Two towels were laid out on the lawn. We had to strip there, then run upstairs to soak in hot baths.

The old people said nothing and were kind to me but did not approve our behaviour. Sheilah was in the dog house, and not for the first time.

I was astonished to discover she was expected to cook for us all in a vast kitchen, dependent on several paraffin stoves set on a long deal table, when at home we had an Aga. It dawned on me that Sheilah was trapped in an unsatisfactory situation, and hadn't found a way of escape. It was obvious she hadn't a bean, and the old Tweedies were not forthcoming so far as money was concerned.

Sheilah did not resemble her mother; I believe she was a replica of her father, and it prejudiced the old Tweedies against her.

Food rationing was still very strict in 1950, and there were no fresh bananas. We ate dried ones, darkish brown, shrunken and tough, but retaining the sweetness everyone craved.

One evening Sheilah placed two dried bananas beside Mrs Tweedie's chair, and I waited in agonised apprehension for what would happen next. The joke was wonderfully funny and realistic, but I was shocked that she had the nerve to rag the old lady in such a way.

Sure enough, Mrs Tweedie came into the drawing-room and sat on her chair, and when she looked down, thought the bananas a dog mess. She let out a yelp, disgusted by its nearness, and even worse when Sheilah ran in and picked up the banana with her fingers. Needless to say the only little dog in the house belonged to Sheilah.

In the train going home I realised my difficulties were less than Sheilah's. I had parents who meant well and gave me enough support to keep me out of poverty. Sheilah's joke was uncharacteristic but perhaps a reflection of desperation.

*　　　*　　　*

Dad's business continued to prosper. He created two directors to lift some of the responsibilities from his shoulders. They were Tony Rotheray, who had married his niece, and David Sowden. Both had been in the Navy and both had survived the terrible Russian Convoys during the Second World War. They were already friends and both more than capable.

Dad thought that they should now take charge of the business and he take a back seat, but when he suggested this to them David confessed he had dreamt of buying a farm for years, and this was the moment he should perhaps resign. This was a body blow for Dad, but to his credit he actually encouraged David to go ahead and went with him on several occasions to look at farms for sale. Their friendship became close and lasted until Dad's death. I know David always appreciated Dad's generosity of spirit and equally his advice, and a lot of good came from it.

I think it was David's resignation that determined Dad's decision to float his company, and finally retire, and fortunately Tony agreed. The flotation was a success and Dad gave us his three daughters a more than generous proportion of the proceeds.

What next? Both Uncle Phil and Dad were born before the turn of the nineteenth century, and I believe that boys of their generation took riding for granted. It was just part of their lives. From letters written after Uncle Phil's death one learned that he had been an outstanding horseman, and I believe that Dad must have been the same. Now, without a word to anyone, he approached Mr Paisley who had an established riding school in Harrogate, and with his help Dad taught himself to both ride and jump, through sheer balance. The severe First World War knee wound had left him lame, one leg two inches shorter than the other, but worse still, the knee had no 'grip.' Somehow he must learn to stay on board.

Dad liked Tom Paisley and it was, I believe, with his help that he taught himself how to ride relying entirely on balance. I had no knowledge of this enterprise. It must have been when I was at the equitation course in Porlock, and as Dad never spoke of it, the subject was never discussed.

When he was ready, he bought a middle-aged hunter called Simon which was sound and steady, but still had a pop in him. He was a splendid hunter and they got on well together, but Dad still had some spectacular falls. Typically, he wore a black coat for a season or two, until he improved his skills. He bought another horse for himself, a great bruising grey of sixteen hands called Barney. He had a tremendous pop in him and never failed Dad's enthusiasm for jumping the most difficult of obstacles.

He chose to hunt with the Bedale which has a large and most wonderful territory, especially the Monday country in the Richmond hills. He discovered he preferred hunting with them rather than the York & Ainsty hounds. Jeremy Graham hunted hounds himself and gave everyone spectacular sport.

Due to his limitations, of which he never spoke, once Dad had pointed Barney towards a fence, they took off, straight as a dye and galloping fast. If anyone or thing got in the way it was scattered to the four winds.

I followed behind, taking a steadier course and fearing Dad would have a crash at any moment. At the end of one day I overheard a couple of friends discussing their day. Both were riding young horses and they were quietly schooling them out hunting, giving them confidence and experience.

"How did you get on today?" asked one.

"Pretty good," came the answer, "just two refusals and one Frank Hirsch!"

Bedale members quickly appreciated the danger and avoided collision, but it was some time before they appreciated the cause of Dad's reckless style. When they did he became greatly respected, and was invited to wear pink.

At first none of the locals knew what to make of Dad, but he had one ally and close friend in Roy Smith, a fellow 'industrial invader' like himself, who shared Dad's passion for hunting.

Roy was younger than Dad but as inexperienced, and he too took some terrible 'purlers', and his permanently concertina'd top hat became quite a landmark. Roy was one of the nicest and kindest men one could meet and had a marvellous sense of humour. He befriended Dad from the start, but even Dad was surprised to learn, after Roy's untimely death, that he had been a double First at Cambridge University. Roy hid his many lights under a bushel.

Le Petit Denantou

SHORTLY AFTER OUR RETURN from Ireland, Aunt Eva's third daughter arrived to take on the job of girl groom. She lived as family and was to be responsible for Dad's hunters and I was to continue to care for Patsy Fagan.

Mickie was a surprise, a tall girl with shoulder length, shining gold hair, she bore no resemblance to her elder sisters whom we had met at Tanrego. Brought up 'in the saddle', she rode naturally and well, and loved hunting. She was certainly up to the job and could muck out, bed down, groom and clean tack six times faster than myself, and do it all without apparent effort.

She cheered up the house, her booming voice smacked echos at its quiet walls She spoke in an exaggerated brogue, and if offered a cup of tea, would laugh and say,

"Oh, yes! And thick enough to run a mouse round the top!" using similar nonsense 'sayings' at every opportunity, and Dad laughed helplessly. Mother and I laughed too for some time.

She went down much better than I in the neighbourhood, and I liked her, but could not help envying her many talents. Mucking out and grooming just about killed me and I felt more and more tired each and every day. I was healthy and strong but had extreme low blood pressure. I had rheumatic bouts when younger too, which probably accounted for my near exhaustion, but perhaps a lack of stimulation was the true problem.

The steep walk from house to stables got harder every day, until I didn't make it. Our family doctor from Harrogate told us that the trouble was a very severe jaundice and I turned bright yellow in the following days. However ill I felt I thought jaundice a bonus. I snuggled down in bed thankful that I didn't have to try and keep up with Mickie.

Dr. Campbell recommended that I should go to Switzerland and recuperate there, and Mummy and I landed up in Champéry. It was the first time I'd been in the mountains and their massive beauty, sparkling in bright sunshine, made me feel almost instantly better. Mother and I took lessons and we both enjoyed skiing; Mummy was careful and cautious, but I fell in love with speed.

Monsieur Fonjala, an old fraud, stayed in the same hotel, keeping an eye on his so called "finishing school young ladies." He oiled up to Mother and suggested that as I was making progress on the slopes and enjoying myself, perhaps it would be a good idea if I stayed on and joined his school in Lausanne.

He promised I'd learn French and take French secretarial lessons and shorthand. What was more, it would give me another fortnight in the mountains, so I need hardly say that I longed to take the opportunity, and Mother agreed. She left me there and returned on her own.

When the time came to leave Champéry, the train journey down from the mountains to Montreux was unforgettable. There were patches of thaw here and there and courageous wild flowers appeared through the cracks. I stood on the little outdoor platform at the back of each carriage for the entire journey, totally enthralled.

We returned to the lower slopes later in the Spring to see wild narcissus fields flowering under pink blossomed apple trees; bees and insects buzzing everywhere and the all pervading scent of flowers.

The school was in Ouchy, a mile or two outside Lausanne,

and called Le Petit Denantou. It was a beautiful old house and its lawns sloped down to a little beach on the side of the Lac. I shared a room with two girls, one from Italy and the other Swedish. They had attended the previous term of that year but not joined in the trip to Champéry, so both spoke good French and this made it easy for me to catch up.

Our room was large with a balcony overhung with wisteria and looking out on the lake and long avenue marked by magnolias, so beautiful when in flower. Later the wisteria filled our bedroom with its unforgettable scent nearly overpowering us, and I have planted wisterias in my pergola today to remind me of that happy time.

I stayed with Giovanna at her family holiday house in the Dolomites at some point, and it was fun. She had two rather more beautiful elder sisters and the family car was hotly pursued by two handsome boyfriends on motorbikes wherever we went. The little mountain roads were untarred, and on arrival their faces were white with stone dust sticking to long eyelashes.

The youngest in the family was a little boy, thoroughly spoilt but still a nice child. He and I went looking for fungi in the forest round their wooden chalet. I picked the mushrooms somewhat unwillingly as they were huge with egg yellow sponge under leather brown caps. But fried, they were spectacularly delicious, and I ate too many and was on the verge of being sick before I realised how rich they were.

Visiting Grandpa on my return to England, I told him how much I had enjoyed Italy and what fun it had been in the Dolomites, and he said,

"That's not Italy! That's Austria, but given to the Italians after the First World War."

I told him how I had travelled alone and met the family at Pisa station. I didn't see them at first, and had to walk a long open platform before finding them, and all the Italian boys whistled as I passed. I wasn't frightened, but Giovanna's father was shocked that I should have travelled on my own, and didn't approve.

Back at school, I was placed in the lowest form with a group of English girls, mostly from Manchester, who had no intention of taking the course seriously. Each night they escaped into town, and most were madly in love with Egyption taxi drivers. At least they came to know the geography of Lausanne down to its last inch which might be of use one day.

Our *institutrice* was Madame Recevoir, a very good teacher utterly frustrated by her pupils' lack of interest, so she descended on me like a ton of bricks, and within a week or two I was finding my way.

My great friend was Marie Antoinette and she was employed to help with the teaching. She came from Paris, again a piece of luck for me since I learned French with a Parisian accent rather than the lugubrious Swiss sound.

She had befriended an old sailor we called Capitaine Feo, and he took us out on the yacht he cared for, and we enjoyed glorious days of swimming and sailing on the lake, gorging ourselves on cherries when in season and very cheap. Neither Marie Antoinette nor I had a penny between us but we could at least afford to buy Feo the cherries! Most of the Mancunians got £10 notes in every letter from home and were never short of cash.

Most weekends we spent with old Feo, and when we passed the school, he used to shake his fist and shout 'Loin des méchants!' and oh what fun it was.

When it dawned on me that Fonjala had no intention of introducing the promised lessons in French shorthand and typing, I walked to the university and discovered they were running a summer course for foreigners, and I applied.

I had to write an essay and chose to describe my crossing the bridge en route to the university in pouring rain, remembering the hundreds of coloured umbrellas disrupting any possible progress, and it got me in. I then found some 'digs' that I thought I could afford if I could persuade old Fonge to repay what was left of Dad's fees for the school term.

Dreadful old Fonjy collapsed when I told him. Oily tears dripped down his fat face and he cried, "Non! Non! Non! ma petite Pamela!"

He said the school would be disgraced if anyone found out, and what would he say to my Father? He looked so like Toad in *The Wind in the Willows* I foolishly felt a bit sorry for him. In the end we agreed a compromise. I would stay on at Denantou but go to the University every day instead of lessons in school. It was a poor agreement on my side, because I could not afford the bus, and the walk was about an hour, and we were badly fed and quite often I nearly fainted before I got there. Somehow I managed, I suppose because I enjoyed being there so much.

I particularly disliked Fonjala's mother. She was a large woman who lived in school with her beloved poodles. After a light lunch of cold meat cut thin and salad, I saw the dogs munching best steak in the kitchens. Madame Fonjala ate her lunch with us students and was served first and always took a very greedy portion of what was offered. One day there were delicious and piping hot French Fries, and a chip fell off the fork and down her ample chest, the divide so deep there was no chance of rescue! "Oh là là! Oh là là!'

she cried out in agony. And secretly we were all delighted.

All too soon the University course came to an end. I had begun to make friends there and hated to leave, and the University invited me stay for another full year to study literature.

At the time I was so grounded in the conviction that my parents needed me at home and also that it would be selfish to ask Dad to fund me yet again for a whole year abroad, that I turned it down.

When I got home I realised how mistaken and how silly was the decision. I found Mummy and Dad were getting along together much better than before, and Mickie was well settled and happy in her job as Dad's girl groom. I should have had more sense and told my parents what had been on offer and how I wished to accept.

After a skiing holiday the following winter, I stayed with Marie Antoinette with her family in Paris en route for home. It was the time when King George VI had died, and the Paris newspapers were full of graphic photographs of the funeral.

Her family were welcoming, and her father and brother both architects whose offices took up part of their very large appartement. We all met in the kitchen for lunch. I understood the family were comfortably well off, so it was a big surprise to discover their economy with lavatory paper. Squares of newspaper was all there was, a very inadequate substitute, and I found it almost impossible to use when it was covered with pictures of our Royal Family's grief, and especially the photograph of the Three Queens.

Marie Antoinette was very special. She was tall with a beautiful bony figure. Her face, with broad forehead below soft waving fair hair, was lit by fine eyes sparkling with intelligence, and her wide mouth possessed a lovely and endearing smile. Perhaps not a classical beauty; in fact much more. Her joy in life and living, her deep love of family, her favourite holidays spent sailing off the Brittany coast, shone through her personality. I loved her deeply and was aware of her distress over falling in love with a delightful Swiss man who was a dedicated Lutheran whilst she was Catholic. Their parents were against the marriage. The divide went deep, and my beloved friend decided to become a nun and I was not allowed to write.

I wish I had kept her address; her parents will have died but one of her siblings might still be there, and surely now I might be allowed to get in touch with her again. Thinking about her now, I realise how much I have missed her; we understood each other well, and she had the sort of common sense that might have saved me from all the idiotic mistakes I made in my life.

*   *   *

My parents welcomed me home to a wonderful party and we danced in Harrogate's smartest hotel . . . but there was only one young man I wanted to dance with, and I soon found out that his interests lay elsewhere.

Dad and Mum left Mickie and myself in charge of the house, while they went off to see Dee and Buffin in South Africa. They had engaged a most unsuitable cook, called Rose, and one day I found her throwing the potato peelings, egg-shells and tea leaves through the scullery window, instead of in the pig bucket. I think it was poor old Bert who had the job of tidying them up. She couldn't cook either, and without further ado I sacked her.

Mickie was a bit difficult too. She was spending a lot of time with Dad's new cowman who lived in the cottage with his young, wife and their two babies. I noticed the wife looked very thin, almost ill, and the children peeped out from behind her skirts and seemed to be frightened. Then one day their mother had a black eye, and I understood the situation.

The cowman had a habit of dropping his false teeth as a joke when one least expected it. Well, I suppose it was a funny kind of shock the first time, but Mickie laughed till she ached every time. This was no good; in some trepidation I spoke to her about it and said she must stop spending time with him, to which she retorted that I should mind my own business and there was nothing in it anyway.

The day before Mum and Dad returned, I saw them both departing with suitcases up the drive.

As usual there was no discussion between Dad and me about what had happened, but neither did he thank me for 'improving', as I thought, the sitting-room fireplace. It certainly looked better, but needed a big wrought iron cover to prevent its smoking, and Dad organised that without any comment.

It was through Uncle Arthur, our doctor in Ilkley, that Mummy discovered Doris. She and her little son John came to cook for us, and Doris was nice and a very good cook.

John was an attractive small person with dark hair and lustrous brown eyes. One day he hid behind the oak chest at the bottom of the stairs and popped out when Dad came down and shouted,

"Stick 'em up!"

It was dark in the hall and Dad got the fright of his life.

"Don't you ever point that gun at anybody ever again!" he announced, "or I shall remove it."

Whereupon the child said, "Well, what's it for?"

Dad was completely nonplussed—there really wasn't any answer to that question.

Doris remained with us for years. Dear Ernest Abbott had retired, and it was Jackie Gill who now delivered the weekly orders from the village shop. Jackie was successful in business, but unlucky in love. Every week he eyed Doris with a longing look, but failed to make up his mind.. The weeks progressed into months and then to years.

Mummy half hoped Jackie would pop the question and make Doris happy but knew how much she would miss her, and didn't think Jackie good enough for her. In the end Jackie married her and they were blessed with a little daughter they called Dawn, sometime later. John went into the Army and was based in Germany. Dad, who was there on business, managed to look him up and they had dinner together. That evening has remained an important memory for John who is now a great supporter of our local British Legion.

Cyprus and marriage

WHEN THE FIRST YORKSHIRE Three Day Event was to be held at Harewood I immediately volunteered to help. I was particularly interested because Sheilah and I were in Porlock in 1948 when the successful Olympic team did much of their training there. The team were to us like stars in a film, living in a wonderful far-off world. At seventeeen I thought of them as demi-gods. I was thrilled to pick up and hand back Robert Rook's 'trees' that fell from his boot one day, but did rather wish he had been the more dashing Bertie Hill, a farmer from Somerset.

The riding part of the Olympics was held in Stockholm and Reg Hindley was our Captain, a man older than the others and kept in reserve. We heard the results of each day on the wireless. The team came through the first day of Dressage quite well and were top after the Cross Country. Bertie Hill had a brilliant round in spite of his horse nearly being brought down by some hole in the ground. The next day the vets pronounced it unfit to compete, and our hearts dropped. Reg must stand in for him. Unlike the younger members of the team, he sat his beautiful hunter in 'old-fashioned' style, sitting well back and jumping on a long rein, perfect for hunting but too slow for the needs of international competition. If our team were to have a chance of winning, he must achieve a fast and faultless round, and everyone wondered whether he could possibly do it. He did—flying round that very forbidding jump course without touching a pole. I can still feel how thrilled we were, and yes, how proud, especially of Reg.

When volunteers were needed at Harewood, I got the

job of being secretary to the overall secretary, a local farmer, subject to being able to type and use shorthand. I accepted and shot off to Oxford to learn at Miss Sprule's Secretarial School which was situated at the Carfax crossroads in the centre of town.

I enjoyed the course and finished just in time for my work at Harewood. Other young volunteers were always dropping in, one of whom had the most wonderful blue eyes I have ever known. When I shut mine at night, they were still there smiling at me and he kept popping by throughout the Trials.

At the end of the Trials, Brook (he of the blue eyes) and I met again locally, and on another occasion in London when we visited Kew Gardens, driving there in his car, as one could do so easily in those days. The traffic stopped at red lights and he leaned across for a light kiss, and it was only when there were loud hoots and honks from behind that we remembered where we were. In the garden Brook looked disarmingly smart in his dark suit and bowler hat and we kissed again, but overhanging twigs from a nearby tree caught the bowler and tipped it off, which greatly amused me.

We told our parents we wanted to be engaged, but for very different reasons they were all against the idea, and his parents insisted that it must be kept secret. My parents said nothing, but I knew they were unhappy about it. Brook's father immediately sent him off on some business in the Far East that would keep him away for at least six months. The idea was obviously ill-judged. We were in love but we did not know each other very well and up until then had moved in different circles. Actually I had never had a 'circle' apart form the friends I met skiing. I knew people out hunting of course, but had never felt I was one of them. Now the chance of finding out more about each other on home ground and being openly engaged was lost.

The situation for Brook was much worse than for me. Stranded in places like Outer Mongolia alone, with no knowledge of the language, trying to create business, friendless for months on end. He was always an avid reader of newspapers which of course were non-existent in such places, and he must have missed having books in the hand. Strangely he took little pleasure in finding out how these faraway peoples lived; their habits, customs and history didn't hold his interest and he hated the strange and unappetising food, mostly rice based.

He wrote endless and wonderful letters always looking forward to returning home and managed somehow or other to have beautiful bouquets of flowers sent to me.

For me, too, life was lonely and Yorkshire very dull. I was delighted when Sheilah wrote to invite me to join her and her friend Liza for a holiday in Cyprus, and left almost immediately.

The girls lived in a flat above the main street in Nicosia and squeezed me in somehow. I remember looking down from high windows and seeing Archbishop Makarios and his entourage processing through the town, far below, his black headgear stiff and upright above the bearded face, the progress slow and deliberate, his long garments and those of his followers all as black as ink and appearing to float about them. The scene held menace, even then.

The Mediterranean warmth, however, wrapped itself round me, and Sheilah and Liza said they were happy for me to stay longer than the arranged fortnight, so I found a job picking carnations at a small commercial garden on a hill across from Mnt. Hilarion. The owners were very nice people and I enjoyed wandering down paths of carnations picking any that were of a size to sell, dreaming myself through the days. The scent of the flowers was sensational in that bright hot sunshine but the heat was terrific too, and for the first time in my life I was always thirsty.

We were allowed, however, to help ourselves to cold tea laced with slices of lemon and honey, which was kept in large bottles in a refrigerater back at the farm. The tea was delicious, and I still make it for myself today and enjoy it hot or cold. I couldn't work there for very long as the carnation season was coming to an end, so found another job working in the offices of the Town Council which was more lucrative but not half as enjoyable.

Sheilah worked for an architect but was also overseeing the building of Mrs Pope's racing stud. Mrs Pope was American, very rich, very beautiful and difficult. Both Sheilah and I met her through knowing her daughter Pat when we were in Porlock. Mother and daughter could not have been more different. Pat was very gentle and rather shy, someone who hid her enormous talent for dressage, patiently teaching both horses and riders how to do it, her powers for the healing of animals and her contemplative order of life all hidden under the proverbial bushel. Meeting friends casually, one could easily fail to take in that Pat was there, but her mother never failed to be the centre of everyone's attention.

I realised Sheilah was in a rather tricky position, caught between builders' protests and Mrs Pope's impatience when we went to the stables one day, and it certainly didn't help the occasion to have an accident. One of the mares was disturbed and unexpectedly lashed out, breaking my wrist. I thought this would put an end to my job, but after a few days I found that

I could type just as well in plaster as out of it, and the exercise actually helped the injury to heal both quickly and well.

When Mrs Pope decided to return to America for a while she arranged for Sheilah to care for her beautiful little house built on a hill near Kyrenia, and we moved in. There were just two bedrooms so I slept on the patio for the rest of my stay and don't remember that it ever rained, and how lovely it was to escape from hot and dusty Nicosia!

We all worked from 7 a.m. till 1 p.m., the rest of the day being free. Most afternoons we took a picnic lunch down to Kyrenia and sunbathed on the 'slab' which was a vast sloping rock forming one side of the deep sea green harbour where we swam. There was a hotel in Kyrenia and an excellently run club that put on dances now and then, and many military people based in Egypt spent their leaves in Kyrenia, so it was an amusing place to be.

One family we came to know lived in an old carob store, converted into a little house. It was actually in a cavity within the natural rock, and wonderfully quiet and cool. The window of their sitting-room had been cut through about two foot of stone, and leaning through the aperture and seeing the lively harbour scene and all its activity below felt like being in two worlds. I wished and wished I could have stayed there for a night or two, it was such a special place.

Some very early mornings Sheilah and I drove down to the racecourse and exercised the horses just for fun. The Turkish grooms were charming and plied us with tiny jars of delicious, syrupy, hot coffee when we came back which helped to keep us awake for the six hours of office work that followed. It also left its unforgettable flavour, which, in my experience has never been matched.

I liked the Turks I met more than the Greeks who always seemed to be rather pleased with themselves, most of them qualified and a bit superior.

We met and made friends with dear Lawrence Eliot, who was an aide to the Governor and I went with him one evening to a film-show outside and under the stars. I remember a full moon and the film very romantic. Since Lawrence was on duty, he and I sat on the front seats immediately behind the Governor. Normally there was a break half way through the film when drinks were served, but on this occasion they failed to turn up, so the programme proceeded and finished some few minutes earlier than usual. Moments after our departure all the front seats were blown sky-high. It was the beginning of the troubles.

I left soon after this, but Liza and Sheilah stayed. Sheilah had acquired a little open Fiat by this time and it was her pride and joy. When there were riots in the street, she became known for sitting on top of it, armed with a truncheon which she used to wield accurately, when necessary, and was successful in defending her territory.

*　　*　　*

Four of the six months had gone and Brook was on his way back to England at last, so I said my goodbyes to Cyprus and friends and as brown as a berry I too flew home. I was pleased with my tan; the few weeks in South Africa hadn't been long enough to make much difference, but constant Cyprus sunshine for months on end had done the trick. I was a bit shocked and very disappointed when Brook's first words were that it didn't suit me! but no real worry, I was back to being pale again in no time thanks to good old Yorkshire weather.

For no reason I can now remember, we planned for a winter

wedding and how different were the arrangements compared with today! Formal invitations were sent out in good time, no wedding present lists, just hundreds of gifts and letters of thanks to write for weeks on end...everything through the post. The presents had to be labelled, showing from whom they came, and must be exhibited at the reception. Dad decided the only place for that was in the billiard room and on top of his beloved billiard table. Mother was in a panic because two exactly matching tea trolleys were amongst the gifts and almost worse, two very expensive hot plates. She and I were miserably worried that the generous givers would be hurt to see their present replicated. In the end she tied the different labels, one at each end of one of them, and prayed the givers might not notice in the crush.

Brook's father gave me a leather suitcase from Aspreys. It had a brown canvas cover to protect the beautiful pigskin of which it was made. Inside it was lined with green kid and fitted with little bowls and bottles which had silver fittings. A beautiful brush, comb and mirror all edged with silver, slotted into the underside of the lid, and the whole thing weighed like lead, but it was very beautiful and I had never beheld anything so smart. When I thanked him, I said it would be perfect for taking with me on our honeymoon, to which he retorted I certainly would not be taking it as it must be there, on display, amongst all the other presents!

My sisters had been married from home and I wanted to do the same. A few days before the ceremony a huge marquee was erected on the grass tennis court, and soon resplendent within with white linen on flower decked tables, it all looked wonderful. Two nights before the wedding however, snow began to fall. We weren't worried at first, we had no memory of really heavy falls before Christmas, but in that year of 1955 the snow continued through the night and never stopped. On the day before the wedding we heard the guy ropes creak.

Dad telephoned the marquee firm and they sent a lorry to the rescue, but the snow continued to fall and the lorry got stuck in drifts on Blubberhouses Moor.

All we could do was to worry and wait, and we were very anxious. The drive was kept clear with constant sweeping so we could get cars up the drive and reach the church, but where Dad thought guests could park their cars for the reception in such conditions I have no idea.

By now we were really worried. The guy ropes continued to complain and then, with a sigh, the whole edifice gently subsided before our eyes.

Mother and Dad and I watched it happen, aghast. We stood together in silence, each with his or her thoughts racing in circles as we wondered if the wedding itself would have to be postponed. Then we noticed a movement in the canvas near where the entrance had been. Something was moving under it and, as we watched, the large behind of a very fat waitress backed into view. Thankful to discover she was unhurt, we began to laugh, and she laughed with us. We had no idea how we would cope next day, but in that moment nothing seemed to be more important than the very nice waitress's reappearance unhurt.

The Red Lion Restaurant in South Stainley more than rose to the occasion. They had been engaged to do the catering and they invited us to have the wedding on their premises. Only guests with Land Rovers managed to reach the Church, but Cooper Atkinson and the Whipper In, dressed in their hunting scarlet, stood each side of the door as we emerged after the service, their hunting whips creating an arch over us. Nearly everyone managed to reach the Red Lion. There was a sense of satisfactory achievement and good cheer all round, and darling Mum said the snow was a mercy in the end, as no one viewed the presents, and she had no need to worry about the duplicate trolleys and hotplates, which incidentally are still in use today.

Sheilah had flown from Cyprus to be at my wedding and on her way back to Petersfield next day she called in on Dick Hern. She had loved Dick from the first moment they met when she and I walked down to the sea on our first day in Porlock. Nine long years had passed since that fatal meeting and I think Sheilah had come to accept a proposal would never happen. Driving down that day she looked forward to seeing him again and having a friendly 'catch up' on news and mutual friends. She was astonished to see champagne ready on the sideboard, and could hardly take in he was asking her to marry him.

Her joyous letter was waiting for me when we came home from our honeymoon and we were thrilled for both of them. A little later we were invited to her wedding in London and of course I went. There was Dick and his best man waiting in the front row as the church filled up with all their friends, and we waited expectantly for Sheilah's arrival. The organ played on and I couldn't help feeling she had a little overplayed the part of keeping her bridegroom waiting. The organ continued to play and everyone became a little restless.

It was a good half hour later that old Mr. Tweedie, her grandfather, guided her up the aisle . Later we learned he had mistakenly taken her to the wrong church. The organ had been playing wedding music so everything seemed alright at first.

They had walked half way up the aisle before seeing another bridal couple ahead of them! They beat a hasty retreat and having paid off their taxi, they had to wait for another…all in all they had made pretty good time in the end.

Life had moved forward and much had happened to all three of us during the nine long years since we first met on the cobbled beach in Porlock, but Sheilah's love for Dick had never wavered. Our lives too grew closer and closer like a tight woven tapestry for the rest of our lives.

Green Howard Brooch

THE FIRST YEAR of my marriage was spent travelling, mostly in the Far East, but coming home was an adventure too. My life filled with surprises, not all of them good.

The little farmhouse, situated in the middle of a village, had been 'smartened up' with swirled white plaster on its lovely old brick walls. Its simple interior had been painted throughout in pale grey-blue, and oatmeal-coloured carpeting was everywhere except in the kitchen. Brook was delighted to have bought the stuff from his brother-in-law who had discovered a new manufacturing process which blew wool tufts on to a sticky rubber backing. It looked good and was very cheap. It enabled the poorest household to throw out the mats and have wall-to-wall. We both loved dogs, and soon had three or four between us, but house-training the pups was disastrous. The smallest spill became a permanent stain, irremovable, and bright yellow.

I said nothing of my dislike of the swirled suburban-looking plaster as I could do nothing about it, but I soon painted and papered the inside of the house, and made the curtains, went to sales, which I loved, and found appropriate furniture.

I found it very odd living in a village after the quiet of a Dale's farm. The blacksmith opposite the green made shoes for horses and mended endless agricultural machinery; all day long the noise of his tapping, but I soon got used to it. I designed a simple garden, and met my neighbours over the low wall. It was all very cheerful and friendly but Brook hated it. He insisted we have a six-foot wall round the property. At least it kept the dogs in, but its height made one feel imprisoned.

174

Today I can feel the happiness of a day spent with my mother. We were sitting on the doorstep of a beautiful Queen Anne house in Spring sunshine, and dreamed what we would do to transform it into a home.

The place was abandoned and in the middle of some hundred flat acres of spring corn; the building itself, turned into a grain store. It had no view, no river, no hill, but the edges of the huge fields were lined by strips of wispy woodland, from which came the sound of a spring chorus. Fat and happy birds were everywhere, and there was no other sound.

The original track to the house had been ploughed in. We had left my car in the lane and walked to the place, but one could still trace where it once had been. The dogs were round us, well exercised and content to lie in the soft sunshine. The little place had once been a farm; there was still a yard with buildings of the same date clustered round it.

In imagination my mother and I saw how they could be turned into a cottage, with stables and barn, accommodation for help that one would need to keep the place in good nick. The main house had four downstairs rooms and four on the first floor. They were beautifully proportioned, with lovely fireplaces, one of which is in the house that I live in today. My second son rescued it and brought it for me secretly. I wonder if he sometimes looks at it and thinks, as I do, of what might have been.

Having planned the accommodation, my mother and I turn our attention to the garden. There is the remnant of a once beautiful orchard that could be pruned back to order, and on that day was full of cherry blossom. The path to the orchard was charged with masses of white violets and, as we sat in that early spring sunshine, their scent was all round us.

I remember turning to my mother and saying, "Why on earth did they not tell me about this place? It is so perfect and would have suited me so much better than our house, slap in the middle of the village! The 'they' were my husband and his family. I had hunted across this land and seen the little house on several occasions without realising that my father-in-law owned it all.

When Brook came home from work that evening the blacksmith across the green was still hard at it and he was irritated by the noise, so I asked him why he had not told me of the little farm and all its possibilities.

"Oh, we thought you would feel too lonely out there," he replied.

As always, everyone meant well but, to my surprise, never thought to discover my views. I no more liked living in the middle of a busy village than he did, but we made the best of it and on the whole enjoyed ourselves. In fact I became very fond of Rose Farm. I came to know and like everyone in the village, and they put up with us and all our dogs, and welcomed us. Yes, we had a happy time there for the most part.

The morning after my mother's visit, the telephone rang.

"Oh darling, when I went to bed last night, I discovered my Green Howard brooch was missing. I know it is a long shot, but could you go back to the house and have a look round?"

"Of course, Mummy, I'll go today." I knew how she loved that brooch. Dad had given it to her when he came home from the war, and she wore it all the time. I thought of us walking across the acres from where we left the car, exploring the house and wandering in its orchard, remembered the thick clumps of violets everywhere; it certainly was a 'long shot.'

I put the dogs in the car, went back and stood in front of

the house where we had sat and looked down on the clustered violets lining the path. 'Oh well, I'd better start somewhere!' Bending, I put my hand down, felt through the violets and found the brooch.

It is odd how this happens when there is something, a place or a person, so bound up in love and joy. All remains well. Whatever is temporarily lost is found again and the memory remains perfect and undefiled.

THE END

Acknowledgements

I'd like to thank the members of the writing group
The Next Chapter for their interest and support, especially
our leader, Jackie Buxton; also Clive Robinson for reading the
first draft; but most of all Michelle Moore who collated my
scattered writings over several years, and without
whose help this book could not have appeared.